The First Man

Eugene O'Neill

DODO PRESS

"THE FIRST MAN"

A PLAY IN FOUR ACTS

BY EUGENE O'NEILL

CHARACTERS

CURTIS JAYSON

MARTHA, his wife

JOHN JAYSON, his father, a banker

JOHN, JR., his brother

RICHARD, his brother

ESTHEE (MRS. MARK SHEFFIELD), his sister

LILY, his sister

MRS. DAVIDSON, his father's aunt

MARK SHEFFIELD, a lawyer

EMILY, JOHN JR. 'S wife

RICHARD BIGELOW

A MAID

A TRAINED NURSE

TIME—The Present

SCENES

ACT I

Living-room in the house of CURTIS JAYSON, Bridgetown, Conn. — an afternoon in early Fall.

ACT II

CURTIS' study—morning of the following day.

ACT III

The same—three o'clock in the morning of a day in early spring of the next year.

ACT IV

Same as Act I—three days later.

The First Man

ACT I

SCENE—Living-room of CURTIS JAYSON'S house in Bridgetown, Conn. A large, comfortable room. On the left, an arm-chair, a big open fireplace, a writing desk with chair in far left corner. On this side there is also a door leading into CURTIS' study. In the rear, center, a double doorway opening on the hall and the entryway. Bookcases are built into the wall on both sides of this doorway. In the far right corner, a grand piano. Three large windows looking out on the lawn, and another arm-chair, front, are on this right side of the room. Opposite the fireplace is a couch, facing front. Opposite the windows on the right is a long table with magazines, reading lamp, etc. Four chairs are grouped about the table. The walls and ceiling are in a French gray color. A great rug covers most of the hardwood floor.

It is around four o'clock of a fine afternoon in early fall.

As the curtain rises, MARTHA, CURTIS and BIGELOW are discovered. MARTHA is a healthy, fine-looking woman of thirty-eight. She does not appear this age for her strenuous life in the open has kept her young and fresh. She possesses the frank, clear, direct quality of outdoors, outspoken and generous. Her wavy hair is a dark brown, her eyes blue-gray. CURTIS JAYSON is a tall, rangy, broad-shouldered man of thirty-seven. While spare, his figure has an appearance of rugged health, of great nervous strength held in reserve. His square-jawed, large-featured face retains an eager boyish enthusiasm in spite of its prevailing expression of thoughtful, preoccupied aloofness. His crisp dark hair is graying at the temples. EDWARD BIGELOW is a large, handsome man of thirty- nine. His face shows culture and tolerance, a sense of humor, a lazy unambitious contentment. CURTIS is reading an article in some scientific periodical, seated by the table. MARTHA and BIGELOW are sitting nearby, laughing and chatting.

BIGELOW—[Is talking with a comically worried but earnest air.] Do you know, I'm getting so I'm actually afraid to leave them alone with that governess. She's too romantic. I'll wager she's got a whole book full of ghost stories, superstitions, and yellow- journal horrors up her sleeve.

MARTHA—Oh, pooh! Don't go milling around for trouble. When I was a kid I used to get fun out of my horrors.

BIGELOW—But I imagine you were more courageous than most of us.

MARTHA—Why?

BIGELOW—Well, Nevada—the Far West at that time—I should think a child would have grown so accustomed to violent scenes—

MARTHA—[Smiling.] Oh, in the mining camps; but you don't suppose my father lugged me along on his prospecting trips, do you? Why, I never saw any rough scenes until I'd finished with school and went to live with father in Goldfield.

BIGELOW—[Smiling.] And then you met Curt.

MARTHA—Yes—but I didn't mean he was a rough scene. He was very mild even in those days. Do tell me what he was like at Cornell.

BIGELOW—A romanticist—and he still is!

MARTHA—[Pointing at CURTIS with gay mischief.] What! That sedate man! Never!

CURTIS—[Looking up and smiling at them both affectionately—lazily.] Don't mind him, Martha. He always was crazy.

BIGELOW—[To CURT—accusingly.] Why did you elect to take up mining engineering at Cornell instead of a classical degree at the Yale of your fathers and brothers? Because you had been reading Bret Harte in prep. school and mistaken him for a modern realist. You devoted four years to grooming yourself for another outcast of Poker Flat. [MARTHA laughs.]

CURTIS—[Grinning.] It was you who were hypnotized by Harte—so much so that his West of the past is still your blinded New England-movie idea of the West at present. But go on. What next?

BIGELOW—Next? You get a job as engineer in that Goldfield mine— but you are soon disillusioned by a laborious life where six-shooters are as rare as nuggets. You try prospecting. You find nothing but different varieties of pebbles. But it is necessary to your nature to project romance into these stones, so you go in strong for geology. As a geologist, you become a slave to the Romance of the Rocks. It is but a step from that to anthropology— the last romance of all. There you find yourself—because there is no further to go. You win fame as the most proficient of young skull-hunters—and wander over the face of the globe, digging up bones like an old dog.

CURTIS—[With a laugh.] The man is mad, Martha.

BIGELOW—Mad! What an accusation to come from one who is even now considering setting forth on a five-year excavating contest in search of the remains of our gibbering ancestor, the First Man!

CURTIS—[With sudden seriousness.] I'm not considering it any longer. I've decided to go.

MARTHA—[Starting—the hurt showing in her voice.] When did you decide?

CURTIS—I only really came to a decision this morning. [With a seriousness that forces BIGELOW'S interested attention.] It's a case of got to go. It's a tremendous opportunity that it would be a crime for me to neglect.

BIGELOW—And a big honor, too, isn't it, to be picked as a member of such a large affair?

CURTIS—[With a smile.] I guess it's just that they want all the men with considerable practical experience they can get. There are bound to be hardships and they know I'm hardened to them. [Turning to his wife with an affectionate smile.] We haven't roughed it in the queer corners for the last ten years without knowing how it's done, have we, Martha?

MARTHA—[Dully.] No, Curt.

CURTIS—[With an earnest enthusiasm.] And this expedition IS what you call a large affair, Big. It's the largest thing of its kind ever undertaken. The possibilities, from the standpoint of anthropology, are limitless.

BIGELOW—[With a grin.] Aha! Now we come to the Missing Link!

CURTIS—[Frowning.] Darn your Barnum and Bailey circus lingo, Big. This isn't a thing to mock at. I should think the origin of man would be something that would appeal even to your hothouse imagination. Modern science believes—knows—that Asia was the first home of the human race. That's where we're going, to the great Central Asian plateau north of the Himalayas.

BIGELOW—[More soberly.] And there you hope to dig up—our first ancestor?

CURTIS—It's a chance in a million, but I believe we may, myself— at least find authentic traces of him so that we can reconstruct his life and habits. I was up in that country a lot while I was mining advisor to the Chinese government—did some of my own work on the side. The extraordinary results I obtained with the little means at my disposal convinced me of the riches yet to be uncovered. The First Man may be among them.

BIGELOW—[Turning to MARTHA.] And you were with him on that Asian plateau?

MARTHA—Yes, I've always been with him.

CURTIS—You bet she has. [He goes over and puts his hand on his wife's shoulder affectionately.] Martha's more efficient than a whole staff of assistants and secretaries. She knows more about what I'm doing than I do half the time. [He turns toward his study.] Well, I guess I'll go in and work some.

MARTHA—[Quietly.] Do you need me now, Curt?

BIGELOW—[Starting up.] Yes, if you two want to work together, why just shoo me—

CURTIS—[Puts both hands on his shoulders and forces him to his seat again.] No. Sit down, Big. I don't need Martha now. [Coming over to her, bends down and kisses her—rather mockingly.] I couldn't deprive Big of an audience for his confessions of a fond parent.

BIGELOW—Aha! Now it's you who are mocking at something you know nothing about. [An awkward silence follows this remark.]

CURTIS—[Frowning.] I guess you're forgetting, aren't you, Big? [He turns and walks into his study, closing the door gently behind him.]

MARTHA—[After a pause—sadly.] Poor Curt.

BIGELOW—[Ashamed and confused.] I had forgotten—

MARTHA—The years have made me reconciled. They haven't Curt. [She sighs—then turns to BIGELOW with a forced smile.] I suppose it's hard for any of you back here to realize that Curt and I ever had any children.

BIGELOW—[After a pause.] How old were they when—?

MARTHA—Three years and two—both girls. [She goes on sadly.] We had a nice little house in Goldfield. [Forcing a smile.] We were very respectable home folks then. The wandering came later, after—It was a Sunday in winter when Curt and I had gone visiting some friends. The nurse girl fell asleep—or something—and the children sneaked out in their underclothes and played in the snow. Pneumonia set in—and a week later they were both dead.

BIGELOW—[Shocked.] Good heavens!

MARTHA—We were real lunatics for a time. And then when we'd calmed down enough to realize—how things stood with us—we swore we'd never have children again—to steal away their memory. It wasn't what you thought—romanticism—that set Curt wandering— and me with him. It was a longing to lose ourselves—to forget. He flung himself with all his power into every new study that interested him. He couldn't keep still, mentally or bodily—and I followed. He needed me—then—so dreadfully!

BIGELOW—And is it that keeps driving him on now?

MARTHA—Oh, no. He's found himself. His work has taken the place of the children.

BIGELOW—And with you, too?

MARTHA—[With a wan smile.] Well, I've helped—all I could. His work has me in it, I like to think—and I have him.

BIGELOW—[Shaking his head.] I think people are foolish to stand by such an oath as you took—forever. [With a smile.] Children are a great comfort in one's old age, I've tritely found.

MARTHA—[Smiling.] Old age!

BIGELOW—I'm knocking at the door of fatal forty.

MARTHA—[With forced gaiety.] You're not very tactful, I must say. Don't you know I'm thirty-eight?

BIGELOW—[Gallantly.] A woman is as old as she looks. You're not thirty yet.

MARTHA—[Laughing.] After that nice remark I'll have to forgive you everything, won't I? [LILY JAYSON comes in from the rear. She is a slender, rather pretty girl of twenty-five. The stamp of college student is still very much about her. She rather insists on a superior, intellectual air, is full of nervous, thwarted energy. At the sight of them sitting on the couch together, her eyebrows are raised.]

LILY—[Coming into the room—breezily.] Hello, Martha. Hello, Big. [They both get up with answering "Hellos. "] I walked right in regardless. Hope I'm not interrupting.

MARTHA—Not at all.

LILY—[Sitting down by the table as MARTHA and BIGELOW resume their seats on the lounge.] I must say it sounded serious. I heard you tell Big you'd forgive him everything, Martha. [Dryly—with a mocking glance at BIGELOW.] You're letting yourself in for a large proposition.

BIGELOW—[Displeased but trying to smile it off.] The past is never past for a dog with a bad name, eh, Lily? [LILY laughs. BIGELOW gets up.] If you want to reward me for my truthfulness, Mrs. Jayson, help me take the kids for an airing in the car. I know it's an imposition but they've grown to expect you. [Glancing at his watch.] By Jove, I'll have to run along. I'll get them and then pick you up here. Is that all right?

MARTHA—Fine.

BIGELOW—I'll run, then. Good-by, Lily. [She nods. BIGELOW goes out rear.]

MARTHA—[Cordially.] Come on over here, Lily.

LILY—[Sits on couch with MARTHA—after a pause—with a smile.] You were forgetting, weren't you?

MARTHA—What?

LILY—That you'd invited all the family over here to tea this afternoon. I'm the advance guard.

MARTHA—[Embarrassed.] So I was! How stupid!

LILY—[With an inquisitive glance at MARTHA'S face but with studied carelessness.] Do you like Bigelow?

MARTHA—Yes, very much. And Curt thinks the world of him.

LILY—Oh, Curt is the last one to be bothered by anyone's morals. Curt and I are the unconventional ones of the family. The trouble with Bigelow, Martha, is that he was too careless to conceal his sins—and that won't go down in this Philistine small town. You have to hide and be a fellow hypocrite or they revenge themselves on you. Bigelow didn't. He flaunted his love-affairs in everyone's face. I used to admire him for it. No one exactly blamed him, in their secret hearts. His wife was a terrible, straitlaced creature. No man could have endured her. [Disgustedly.] After her death he suddenly acquired a bad conscience. He'd never noticed the children before. I'll bet he didn't even know their names. And then, presto, he's about in our midst giving an imitation of a wet hen with a brood of ducks. It's a bore, if you ask me.

MARTHA—[Flushing.] I think it's very fine of him.

LILY—[Shaking her head.] His reform is too sudden. He's joined the hypocrites, I think.

MARTHA—I'm sure he's no hypocrite. When you see him with the children—

LILY—Oh, I know he's a good actor. Lots of women have been in love with him. [Then suddenly.] You won't be furious if I'm very, very frank, will you, Martha?

MARTHA—[Surprised.] No, of course not, Lily.

LILY—Well, I'm the bearer of a message from the Jayson family.

MARTHA—[Astonished.] A message? For me?

LILY—Don't think that I have anything to do with it. I'm only a Victor record of their misgivings. Shall I switch it going? Well, then, father thinks, brother John and wife, sister Esther and husband all think that you are unwisely intimate with this same Bigelow.

MARTHA—[Stunned.] I? Unwisely intimate—? [Suddenly laughing with amusement.] Well, you sure are funny people!

LILY—No, we're not funny. We'd be all right if we were. On the contrary, we're very dull and deadly. Bigelow really has a villainous rep. for philandering. But, of course, you didn't know that.

MARTHA—[Beginning to feel resentful—coldly.] No, I didn't—and I don't care to know it now.

LILY—[Calmly.] I told them you wouldn't relish their silly advice. [In a very confidential, friendly tone.] Oh, I hate their narrow small-town ethics as much as you do, Martha. I sympathize with you, indeed I do. But I have to live with them and so, for comfort's sake, I've had to make compromises. And you're going to live in our midst from now on, aren't you? Well then, you'll have to make compromises, too—if you want any peace.

MARTHA—But-compromises about what? [Forcing a laugh.] I refuse to take it seriously. How anyone could think—it's too absurd.

LILY—What set them going was Big's being around such an awful lot the weeks Curt was in New York, just after you'd settled down here. You must acknowledge he was-very much present then, Martha.

MARTHA—But it was on account of his children. They were always with him.

LILY—The town doesn't trust this sudden fond parenthood, Martha. We've known him too long, you see.

MARTHA—But he's Curt's oldest and best friend.

LILY—We've found they always are.

MARTHA—[Springing to her feet—indignantly.] It's a case of evil minds, it seems to me—and it would be extremely insulting if I didn't have a sense of humor. [Resentfully.] You can tell your family, that as far as I'm concerned, the town may—

LILY—Go to the devil. I knew you'd say that. Well, fight the good fight. You have all my best wishes. [With a sigh.] I wish I had something worth fighting for. Now that I'm through with college, my occupation's gone. All I do is read book after book. The only live people are the ones in books, I find, and the only live life.

MARTHA—[Immediately sympathetic.] You're lonely, that's what, Lily.

LILY—[Drily.] Don't pity me, Martha—or I'll join the enemy.

MARTHA—I'm not. But I'd like to help you if I could. [After a pause.] Have you ever thought of marrying?

LILY—[With a laugh.] Martha! How banal! The men I see are enough to banish that thought if I ever had it.

MARTHA—Marriage isn't only the man. It's children. Wouldn't you like to have children?

LILY—[Turning to her bluntly.] Wouldn't you?

MARTHA—[Confused.] But—Lily—

LILY—Oh, I know it wasn't practicable as long as you elected to wander with Curt—but why not now when you've definitely settled down here? I think that would solve things all round. If you could present Father with a grandson, I'm sure he'd fall on your neck. He feels piqued at the John and Esther families because they've had a run of girls. A male Jayson! Aunt Davidson would weep with joy. [Suddenly.] You're thirty-eight, aren't you, Martha?

MARTHA—Yes. LILY—Then why don't you—before it's too late? [MARTHA, struggling with herself, does not answer. LILY goes on slowly.] You won't want to tag along with Curt to the ends of the earth forever, will you? [Curiously.] Wasn't that queer life like any other? I mean, didn't it get to pall on you?

MARTHA—[As if confessing it reluctantly.] Yes—perhaps—in the last two years.

LILY—[Decisively.] It's time for both of you to rest on your laurels. Why can't Curt keep on with what he's doing now—stay home and write his books?

MARTHA—Curt isn't that kind. The actual work—the romance of it— that's his life.

LILY—But if he goes and you have to stay, you'll be lonesome—[meaningly] alone.

MARTHA—Horribly. I don't know what I'll do.

LILY—Then why—why? Think, Martha. If Curt knew—that was to happen—he'd want to stay here with you. I'm sure he would.

MARTHA—[Shaking her head sadly.] No. Curt has grown to dislike children. They remind him of—ours that were taken. He adored them so—he's never become reconciled.

LILY—If you confronted Curt with the actual fact, he'd be reconciled soon enough, and happy in the bargain.

MARTHA—[Eagerly.] Do you really think so?

LILY—And you, Martha—I can tell from the way you've talked that you'd like to.

MARTHA—[Excitedly.] Yes, I—I never thought I'd ever want to again. For many years after they died I never once dreamed of it—But lately—the last years—I've felt—and when we came to live here—and I saw all around me—homes—and children, I—[She hesitates as if ashamed at having confessed so much.]

LILY—[Putting an arm around her—affectionately.] I know. [Vigorously.] You must, that's all there is to it! If you want my advice, you go right ahead and don't tell Curt until it's a fact he'll have to learn to like, willy-nilly. You'll find, in his inmost heart, he'll be tickled to death.

MARTHA—[Forcing a smile.] Yes, I—I'll confess I thought of that. In spite of my fear, I—I've—I mean—I—[She flushes in a shamed confusion.]

LILY—[Looking at her searchingly.] Why, Martha, what—[Then suddenly understanding—with excited pleasure.] Martha! I know! It is so, isn't it? It is!

MARTHA—[In a whisper.] Yes.

LILY—[Kissing her affectionately.] You dear, you! [Then after a pause.] How long have you known?

MARTHA—For over two months. [There is a ring from the front door bell in the hall.]

LILY—[Jumping up.] I'll bet that's we Jaysons now. [She runs to the door in the rear and looks down the hall to the right.] Yes, it's Esther and husband and Aunt Davidson. [She comes back to MARTHA laughing excitedly. The MAID is seen going to the door.] The first wave of attack, Martha! Be brave! The Young Guard dies but never surrenders!

MARTHA—[Displeased but forcing a smile.] You make me feel terribly ill at ease when you put it that way, Lily. [She rises now and goes to greet the visitors, who enter. MRS. DAVIDSON is seventy-five years old—a thin, sinewy old lady, old-fashioned, unbending and rigorous in manner. She is dressed aggressively in the fashion of a bygone age. ESTHER is a stout, middle-aged woman with the round, unmarked, sentimentally—contented face of one who lives unthinkingly from day to day, sheltered in an assured position in her little world. MARK, her husband, is a lean, tall, stooping man of about forty-five. His long face is alert, shrewd, cautious, full of the superficial craftiness of the lawyer mind. MARTHA kisses the two women, shakes hands with MARK, uttering the usual meaningless greetings in a forced tone. They reply in much the same spirit. There is the buzz of this empty chatter while MARTHA gets them seated.

LILY stands looking on with a cynical smile of amusement. MRS. DAVIDSON is in the chair at the end of table, left, ESTHER sits by MARTHA on couch, MARK in chair at front of table.] Will you have tea now or shall we wait for the others?

ESTHER—Let's wait. They ought to be here any moment.

LILY—[Maliciously.] Just think, Martha had forgotten you were coming. She was going motoring with Bigelow. [There is a dead silence at this—broken diplomatically by SHEFFIELD.]

SHEFFIELD—Where is Curt, Martha?

MARTHA—Hard at work in his study. I'm afraid he's there for the day. SHEFFIELD—[Condescendingly.] Still plugging away at his book, I suppose. Well, I hope it will be a big success.

LILY—[Irritated by his smugness.] As big a success as the brief you're writing to restrain the citizens from preventing the Traction Company robbing them, eh Mark? [Before anyone can reply, she turns suddenly on her aunt who is sitting rigidly on her chair, staring before her stonily like some old lady in a daguerreotype—in a loud challenging tone.] You don't mind if I smoke, Aunt? [She takes a cigarette out of case and lights it.]

ESTHER—[Smiling.] Lily!

MRS. DAVIDSON—[Fixes LILY with her stare—in a tone of irrevocable decision.] We'll get you married, young lady, and that very soon. What you need to bring you down to earth is a husband and the responsibility of children. [Turning her glance to MARTHA, a challenge in her question.] Every woman who is able should have children. Don't you believe that, Martha Jayson? [She accentuates the full name.]

MARTHA—[Taken aback for a moment but restraining her resentment— gently.] Yes, I do, Mrs. Davidson.

MES. DAVIDSON—[Seemingly placated by this reply—in a milder tone.] You must call me aunt, my dear. [Meaningly.] All the Jaysons do.

MARTHA—[Simply.] Thank you, aunt.

LILY—[As if all of this aroused her irritation—in a nervous fuming.] Why don't the others come, darn 'em? I'm dying for my tea. [The door from the study is opened and CURT appears. They all greet him.]

CURTIS—[Absent-mindedly.] Hello, everybody. [Then with a preoccupied air to MARTHA.] Martha, I don't want to interrupt you— but—

MARTHA—[Getting up briskly.] You want my help?

CURTIS—[With the same absent-minded air.] Yes—not for long—just a few notes before I forget them. [He goes back into the study.]

MARTHA—[Seemingly relieved by this interruption and glad of the chance it gives to show them her importance to CURT.] You'll excuse me for a few moments, all of you, won't you? [They all nod.]

MRS. DAVIDSON—[Rather harshly.] Why doesn't Curt hire a secretary? That is no work for his wife.

MARTHA—[Quietly.] A paid secretary could hardly give the sympathy and understanding Curt needs, Mrs. Davidson. [Proudly.] And she would have to study for years, as I have done, in order to take my place. [To LILY.] If I am not here by the time the others arrive, will you see about the tea, Lily—?

LILY—[Eagerly.] Sure. I love to serve drinks. If I were a man, I'd be a bartender—in Mexico or Canada.

MARTHA—[Going toward the study.] I'll be with you again in a minute, I hope. [She goes in and shuts the door behind her.]

ESTHER—[Pettishly.] Even people touched by a smattering of science seem to get rude, don't they?

MRS. DAVIDSON—[Harshly.] I have heard much silly talk of this being an age of free women, and I have always said it was tommyrot. [Pointing to the study.] She is an example. She is more of a slave to Curt's hobbies than any of my generation were to anything but their children. [Still more harshly.] Where are her children?

LILY—They died, Aunt, as children have a bad habit of doing. [Then meaningly.] However, I wouldn't despair if I were you. [MRS. DAVIDSON stares at her fixedly.]

ESTHER—[Betraying a sudden frightened jealousy.] What do you mean, Lily? What are you so mysterious about? What did she say? What—?

LILY—[Mockingly.] Mark, your frau seems to have me on the stand. Can I refuse to answer? [There is a ring at the bell. LILY jumps to her feet excitedly.] Here comes the rest of our Grand Fleet. Now I'll have my tea. [She darts out to the hallway.]

ESTHER—[Shaking her head.] Goodness, Lily is trying on the nerves. [JAYSON, his two sons, JOHN and DICK, and JOHN's wife, EMILY, enter from hallway in rear. JAYSON, the father, is a short, stout, bald-headed man of sixty. A typical, small-town, New England best-family banker, reserved in pose, unobtrusively important—a placid exterior hiding querulousness and a fussy temper. JOHN JUNIOR is his father over again in appearance, but pompous, obtrusive, purse-and-family-proud, extremely irritating in his self-complacent air of authority, emptily assertive and loud. He is about forty. RICHARD, the other brother, is a typical young Casino and country club member, college-bred, good looking, not unlikable. He has been an officer in the war and has not forgotten it. EMILY, JOHN JR. 's wife, is one of those small, mouse-like women who conceal beneath an outward aspect of gentle, unprotected innocence a very active envy, a silly pride, and a mean malice. The people in the room with the exception of MRS. DAVIDSON rise to greet them. All exchange familiar, perfunctory greetings. SHEFFIELD relinquishes his seat in front of the table to JAYSON, going to the chair, right front, himself. JOHN and DICK take the two chairs to the rear of table. EMILY joins ESTHER on the couch and they whisper together excitedly, ESTHER doing most of the talking. The men remain in uncomfortable silence for a moment.]

DICK—[With gay mockery.] Well, the gang's all here. Looks like the League of Nations. [Then with impatience.] Let's get down to cases, folks. I want to know why I've been summoned here. I'm due for tournament mixed-doubles at the Casino at five. Where's the tea—and has Curt a stick in the cellar to put in it?

LILY—[Appearing in the doorway.] Here's tea—but no stick for you, sot. [The MAID brings in tray with tea things.]

JOHN—[Heavily.] It seems it would be more to the point to inquire where our hostess—

JAYSON—[Rousing himself again.] Yes. And where is Curt?

LILY—Working at his book. He called Martha to take notes on something.

ESTHER—[With a trace of resentment.] She left us as if she were glad of the excuse.

LILY—Stuff, Esther! She knows how much Curt depends on her—and we don't.

EMILY—[In her quiet, lisping voice—with the most innocent air.] Martha seems to be a model wife. [But there is some quality to the way she says it that makes them all stare at her uneasily.]

LILY—[Insultingly.] How well you say what you don't mean, Emily! Twinkle, twinkle, little bat! But I'm forgetting to do the honors. Tea, everybody? [Without waiting for any answer.] Tea, everybody! [The tea is served.]

JAYSON—[Impatiently.] Stop fooling, Lily. Let's get to our muttons. Did you talk with Martha?

LILY—[Briskly.] I did, sir.

JAYSON—[In a lowered voice.] What did she say?

LILY—She said you could all go to the devil! [They all look shocked and insulted. LILY enjoys this, then adds quietly.] Oh, not in those words. Martha is a perfect lady. But she made it plain she will thank you to mind your own business.

ESTHER—[Volubly.] And just imagine, she'd even forgotten she'd asked us here this afternoon and was going motoring with Bigelow.

LILY—With his three children, too, don't forget.

EMILY—[Softly.] They have become such well-behaved and intelligent children, they say. [Again all the others hesitate, staring at her suspiciously.]

LILY—[Sharply.] You'd better let Martha train yours for a while, Emily. I'm sure she'd improve their manners—though, of course, she couldn't give them any intelligence.

EMILY—[With the pathos of outraged innocence.] Oh!

DICK—[Interrupting.] So it's Bigelow you're up in the air about? [He gives a low whistle—then frowns angrily.] The deuce you say!

LILY—[Mockingly.] Look at our soldier boy home from the wars getting serious about the family honor! It's too bad this is a rough, untutored country where they don't permit dueling, isn't it, Dick?

DICK—[His pose crumbling—angrily.] Go to the devil!

SHEFFIELD—[With a calm, judicious air.] This wrangling is getting us nowhere. You say she was resentful about our well-meant word to the wise? JAYSON—[Testily.] Surely she must realize that some consideration is due the position she occupies in Bridgetown as Curt's wife.

LILY—Martha is properly unimpressed by big frogs in tiny puddles. And there you are.

MRS. DAVIDSON—[Outraged.] The idea! She takes a lot upon herself— the daughter of a Wild Western coal-miner.

LILY—[Mockingly.] Gold miner, Aunt.

MRS. DAVIDSON—It makes no difference—a common miner! SHEFFIELD— [Keenly inquisitive.] Just before the others came, Lily, you gave out some hints—very definite hints, I should say—

ESTHER—[Excitedly.] Yes, you did, Lily. What did you mean?

LILY—[Uncertainly.] Perhaps I shouldn't have. It's not my secret. [Enjoying herself immensely now that she holds the spotlight— after a pause, in a stage whisper.] Shall I tell you? Yes, I can't help telling.

Well, Martha is going to have a son. [They are all stunned and flabbergasted and stare at her speechlessly.]

MRS. DAVIDSON—[Her face lighting up—joyously.] A son! Curt's son!

JAYSON—[Pleased by the idea but bewildered.] A son?

DICK—[Smartly.] Lily's kidding you. How can she know it's a son— unless she's a clairvoyant.

ESTHER—[With glad relief.] Yes, how stupid!

LILY—I am clairvoyant in this case. Allah is great and it will be a son—if only to make you and Emily burst with envy among your daughters.

ESTHER—Lily!

EMILY—Oh!

JAYSON—[Testily.] Keep still for a moment, Lily, for God's sake. This is no subject to joke about, remember.

LILY—Martha told me. I know that.

JAYSON—And does Curt know this?

LILY—No, not yet. Martha has been afraid to tell him.

JAYSON—Ah, that explains matters. You know I asked Curt some time ago—and he said it was impossible.

EMILY—[With a lift of her eyebrows.] Impossible? Why, what a funny thing to say.

SHEFFIELD—[Keenly lawyer-like.] And why is Martha afraid to tell him, Lily?

LILY—It's all very simple. When the two died years ago, they said they would never have one again. Martha thinks Curt is still haunted by their memory and is afraid he will resent another as an intruder. I told her that was all foolishness—that a child was the one thing to make Curt settle down for good at home here and write his books.

JAYSON—[Eagerly.] Yes, I believe that myself. [Pleased.] Well, this is fine news.

EMILY—Still it was her duty to tell Curt, don't you think? I don't see how she could be afraid of Curt—for those reasons. [They all stare at her.]

ESTHER—[Resentfully.] I don't, either. Why, Curt's the biggest-hearted and kindest—

EMILY—I wonder how long she's known—this?

LILY—[Sharply.] Two months, she said.

EMILY—Two months? [She lets this sink in.]

JOHN—[Quickly scenting something—eagerly.] What do you mean, Emily? [Then as if he read her mind.] Two months? But before that— Curt was away in New York almost a month!

LILY—[Turning on EMILY fiercely.] So! You got someone to say it for you as you always do, Poison Mind! Oh, I wish the ducking stool had never been abolished!

EMILY—[Growing crimson—falteringly.] I—I didn't mean—

JOHN—[Furiously.] Where the honor of the family is at stake—

LILY—[Fiercely.] Ssshh, you empty barrel! I think I hear—[The door from the study is opened and MARTHA comes in in the midst of a heavy silence. All the gentlemen rise stiffly. MARTHA is made immediately self-conscious and resentful by the feeling that they have been discussing her unfavorably.]

MARTHA—[Coming forward—with a forced cordiality.] How do you do, everybody? So sorry I wasn't here when you came. I hope Lily made proper excuses for me. [She goes from one to the other of the four latest comers with "So glad you came, " etc. They reply formally and perfunctorily. MARTHA finally finds a seat on the couch between EMILY and ESTHER.] I hope Lily—but I see you've all had tea.

LILY—[Trying to save the situation—gayly.] Yes. You can trust me as understudy for the part of hostess any time.

MARTHA—[Forcing a smile.] Well, I'm glad to know I wasn't missed.

EMILY—[Sweetly.] We were talking about you—at least, we were listening to Lily talk about you.

MARTHA—[Stiffening defensively.] About me?

EMILY—Yes—about how devoted you were to Curt's work. [LILY gives her a venomous glance of scorn.]

MARTHA—[Pleased but inwardly uneasy.] Oh, but you see I consider it my work, too, I've helped him with it so long now.

JAYSON—[In a forced tone.] And how is Curt's book coming, Martha?

MARTHA—[More and more stung by their strained attitudes and inquisitive glances. Coldly and cuttingly.] Finely, thank you. The book will cause quite a stir, I believe. It will make the name of Jayson famous in the big world outside of Bridgetown.

MRS. DAVIDSON—[Indignantly.] The name of Jayson has been—

JAYSON—[Pleadingly.] Aunt Elizabeth!

LILY—Aunt means it's world famous already, Martha. [Pointing to the sullen JOHN.] John was once a substitute on the Yale Freshman soccer team, you know. If it wasn't for his weak shins he would have made the team, fancy!

DICK—[This tickles his sense of humor and he bursts into laughter.] Lily wins! [As his brother glares at him—looking at his watch.] Heavens, I'll have to hustle! [Gets to his feet.] I'm due at the Casino. [Comes and shakes MARTHA's hand formally.] I'm sorry I can't stay.

MARTHA—So glad you came. Do come in again any time. We keep open house, you know—Western fashion. [She accentuates this.]

DICK—[Hurriedly.] Delighted to. [He starts for the door in rear.]

LILY—[As if suddenly making up her mind.] Wait a second! I'm coming with you—

DICK—Sure thing—only hurry, darn you! [He goes out.]

LILY—[Stops at the door in rear and catching MARTHA's eye, looks meaningly at the others.] Phew! I need fresh air! [She makes an encouraging motion as if pummeling someone to MARTHA, indicating her assembled family as the victim—then goes out laughing. A motor is heard starting—running off.]

ESTHER—[With a huge sigh of relief.] Thank goodness, she's gone. What a vixen! What would you do if you had a sister like that, Martha?

MARTHA—I'd love her—and try to understand her.

SHEFFIELD—[Meaningly.] She's a bad ally to rely on—this side of the fence one day, and that the next.

MARTHA—Is that why you advised her to become a lawyer, Mr. Sheffield?

SHEFFIELD—[Stung, but maintaining an unruffled front.] Now, now, that remark must be catalogued as catty.

MARTHA—[Defiantly.] It seems to be in the Bridgetown atmosphere. I never was—not the least bit—in the open air.

JAYSON—[Conciliatingly.] Oh, Bridgetown isn't so bad, Martha, once you get used to us.

JOHN—It's one of the most prosperous and wealthy towns in the U.S.—and that means in the world, nowadays.

EMILY—[With her sugary smile.] That isn't what Martha means, you silly. I know what she's thinking about us, and I'm not sure that I don't agree with her—partly. She feels that we're so awfully strict—about certain things. It must be so different in the Far West—I suppose—so much freer.

MARTHA—[Acidly.] Then you believe broad-mindedness and clean thinking are a question of locality? I can't agree with you. I know nothing of the present Far West, not having lived there for ten years, but Curt and I have lived in the Far East and I'm sure he'd agree with me in saying that Chinese ancestor worship is far more dignified than ours. After all, you know, theirs is religion, not snobbery. [There is a loud honking of an auto horn before the house. MARTHA starts, seems to come to a quick decision, and announces with studied carelessness.] That must be Mr. Bigelow. I suppose Lily told you I had an engagement to go motoring with him. So sorry I must leave. But I'm like Lily. I need fresh air. [She walks to the study door as she is talking.] I'll call Curt. [She raps loudly on the door and calls.] Curt! Come out! It's important. [She turns and goes to the door, smiling fixedly.] He'll be out when he's through swearing. [She goes out, rear.]

JOHN—[Exploding.] Well, of all the damned cheek!

ESTHER—She shows her breeding, I must say.

EMILY—[With horror.] Oh, how rude—and insulting.

MRS. DAVIDSON—[Rising rigidly to her feet.] I will never set foot in this house again! JAYSON—[Jumping up to restrain her—worriedly.] Now, Aunt Elizabeth, do keep your head! We must have no scandal of any sort. Remember there are servants about. Do sit down. [The old lady refuses in stubborn silence.]

SHEFFIELD—[Judiciously.] One must make allowances for one in her condition, Aunt.

JAYSON—[Snatching at this.] Exactly. Remember her condition. Aunt [testily] and do sit down. [The old lady plumps herself down again angrily.]

EMILY—[In her lisp of hidden meanings.] Yes, the family mustn't forget—her condition. [The door from the study is opened and CURT appears. His face shows his annoyance at being interrupted, his eyes are preoccupied. They all turn and greet him embarrassedly. He nods silently and comes slowly down front.]

CURTIS—[Looking around.] Where's Martha? What's the important thing she called me out for?

ESTHER—[Forcing gaiety.] To play host, you big bear, you! Don't you think we came to see you, too? Sit down here and be good. [He sits on sofa.]

EMILY—[Softly.] Martha had to leave us to go motoring with Mr. Bigelow.

ESTHER—[Hastily.] And the three children.

CURTIS—[Frowning grumpily.] Hm! Big and his eternal kids. [He sighs. They exchange meaning glances. CURT seems to feel ashamed of his grumpiness and tries to fling it off—with a cheerful smile.] But what the deuce! I must be getting selfish to grudge Martha her bit of fresh air. You don't know what it means to outdoor animals like us to be pent up. [He springs to his feet and paces back and forth nervously.] We're used to living with the sky for a roof—[Then interestedly.] Did Martha tell you I'd definitely decided to go on the five year Asian expedition?

ESTHER—Curt! You're not!

EMILY—And leave Martha here—all alone—for five years?

JAYSON—Yes, you can't take Martha with you this time, you know.

CURTIS—[With a laugh.] No? What makes you so sure of that? [As they look mystified, he continues confidentially.] I'll let you in on the secret—only you must all promise not to breathe a word to Martha—until to-morrow. To-morrow is her birthday, you know, and this is a surprise I've saved for her. [They all nod.] I've been intriguing my damnedest for the past month to get permission for Martha to go with me. It was difficult because women are supposed to be barred. [Happily.] But I've succeeded. The letter came this morning. How tickled to death she'll be when she hears! I know she's given up hope. [Thoughtfully.] I suppose it's that has been making her act so out-of-sorts lately.

JAYSON—[Worriedly.] Hmm! But would you persist in going—alone— if you knew it was impossible for her—?

CURTIS—[Frowning.] I can't imagine it without her. You people can't have any idea what a help—a chum—she's been. You can't believe that a woman could be—so much that—in a life of that kind—how I've grown to depend on her. The thousand details—she attends to them all. She remembers everything. Why, I'd be lost. I wouldn't know how to start. [With a laugh.] I know this sounds like a confession of weakness but it's true just the same. [Frowning again.] However, naturally my work must always be the first consideration. Yes, absolutely! [Then with glad relief.] But what's the use of rambling on this way? We can both go, thank heaven!

MRS. DAVIDSON—[Sternly.] No. SHE cannot go. And it is YOUR duty—

CURTIS—[Interrupting her with a trace of impatience.] Oh, come! That's all nonsense, Aunt. You don't understand the kind of woman Martha is.

MRS. DAVIDSON—[Harshly.] The women I understand prefer rearing their children to selfish gallivanting over the world.

CURTIS—[Impatiently.] But we have no children now, Aunt.

MRS. DAVIDSON—I know that, more's the pity. But later—

CURTIS—[Emphatically.] No, I tell you! It's impossible!

MRS. DAVIDSON—[Grimly.] I have said my last word. Go your own road and work your own ruin.

CURTIS—[Brusquely.] I think I'll change my togs and go for a walk. Excuse me for a second. I'll be right down again. [He goes out, rear.]

EMILY—[With her false air of innocence.] Curt acts so funny, doesn't he? Did you notice how emphatic he was about its being impossible? And he said Martha seemed to him to be acting queer lately—with him, I suppose he meant.

ESTHER—He certainly appeared put out when he heard she'd gone motoring with Big.

JAYSON—[Moodily.] This dislike of the very mention of children. It isn't like Curt, not a bit.

JOHN—There's something rotten in Denmark somewhere. This family will yet live to regret having accepted a stranger—

SHEFFIELD—[Mollifyingly—with a judicial air.] Come now! This is all only suspicion. There is no evidence; you have no case; and the defendant is innocent until you have proved her guilty, remember. [Getting to his feet.] Well, let's break up. Esther, you and I ought to be getting home. [They all rise.]

JAYSON—[Testily.] Well, if I were sure it would all blow over without any open scandal, I'd offer up a prayer of thanks.

[The Curtain Falls]

ACT II

SCENE—CURTIS JAYSON'S study. On the left, forward, a gun rack in which are displayed several varieties of rifles and shotguns. Farther back, three windows looking out on the garden. In the rear wall, an open fireplace with two leather arm-chairs in front of it. To right of fireplace, a door leading into the living-room. In the far right corner, another chair. In the right wall, three windows looking out on the lawn and garden. On this side, front, a typewriting table with machine and chair. Opposite the windows on the right, a bulky leather couch, facing front. In front of the windows on the left, a long table with stacks of paper piled here and there on it, reference books, etc. On the left of table, a swivel chair. Gray oak bookcases are built into the cream rough plaster walls which are otherwise almost hidden from view by a collection of all sorts of hunter's trophies, animal heads of all kinds. The floor is covered with animal skins—tiger, polar bear, leopard, lion, etc. Skins are also thrown over the backs of the chairs. The sections of the bookcase not occupied by scientific volumes have been turned into a specimen case for all sorts of zoological, geological, anthropological oddities.

It is mid-morning, sunny and bright, of the following day.

CURTIS and BIGELOW are discovered. CURTIS is half-sitting on the corner of the table, left, smoking a pipe. BIGELOW is lying sprawled on the couch. Through the open windows on the right come the shouts of children playing. MARTHA's voice joins in with theirs.

BIGELOW—Listen to that rumpus, will you! The kids are having the time of their lives. [He goes to the window and looks out—delightedly.] Your wife is playing hide and seek with them. Come and look.

CURTIS—[With a trace of annoyance.] Oh, I can see well enough from here.

BIGELOW—[With a laugh.] She seems to get as much fun out of it as they do. [As a shriek comes from outside—excitedly.] Ah, Eddy discovered her behind the tree. Isn't he tickled now! [He turns back from the window and lights a cigarette—enthusiastically.] Jove, what a hand she is with children!

CURTIS—[As if the subject bored him.] Oh, Martha gets along well with anyone.

BIGELOW—[Sits on the couch again—with a sceptical smile.] You think so? With everyone?

CURTIS—[Surprised.] Yes—with everyone we've ever come in contact with—even aboriginal natives.

BIGELOW—With the aboriginal natives of Bridgetown? With the well- known Jayson family, for example?

CURTIS—[Getting to his feet—frowning.] Why, everything's all right between Martha and them, isn't it? What do you mean, Big? I certainly imagined—but I'll confess this damn book has had me so preoccupied—

BIGELOW—Too darn preoccupied, if you'll pardon my saying so. It's not fair to leave her to fight it alone.

CURTIS—[Impatiently.] Fight what? Martha has a sense of humor. I'm sure their petty prejudices merely amuse her.

BIGELOW—[Sententiously.] A mosquito is a ridiculous, amusing creature, seen under a microscope; but when a swarm has been stinging you all night—

CURTIS—[A broad grin coming over his face.] You speak from experience, eh?

BIGELOW—[Smiling.] You bet I do. Touch me anywhere and you'll find a bite. This, my native town, did me the honor of devoting its entire leisure attention for years to stinging me to death.

CURTIS—Well, if I am to believe one-tenth of the family letters I used to receive on the subject of my old friend, Bigelow, they sure had just cause.

BIGELOW—Oh, I'll play fair. I'll admit they did—then. But it's exasperating to know they never give you credit for changing—I almost said, reforming, One ought to be above the gossip of a town like this—but say what you like, it does get under your skin.

CURTIS—[With an indulgent smile.] So you'd like to be known as a reformed character, eh?

BIGELOW—[Rather ruefully.] Et tu! Your tone is sceptical. But I swear to you, Curt, I'm an absolutely new man since my wife's death, since I've grown to love the children. Before that I hardly knew them. They were hers, not mine, it seemed. [His face lighting up.] Now we're the best of pals, and I've commenced to appreciate life from a different angle. I've found a career at last—the children—the finest career a man could have, I believe.

CURTIS—[Indifferently.] Yes, I suppose so—if you're made that way.

BIGELOW—Meaning you're not?

CURTIS—Not any more. [Frowning.] I tried that once.

BIGELOW—[After a pause—with a smile.] But we're wandering from the subject of Martha versus the mosquitoes.

CURTIS—[With a short laugh.] Oh, to the deuce with that! Trust Martha to take care of herself. Besides, I'll have her out of this stagnant hole before so very long—six months, to be exact.

BIGELOW—Where do you think of settling her then?

CURTIS—No settling about it. I'm going to take her with me.

BIGELOW—[Surprised.] On the Asian expedition?

CURTIS—Yes. I haven't told her yet but I'm going to to-day. It's her birthday—and I've been saving the news to surprise her with.

BIGELOW—Her birthday? I wish the children and I had known—but it's not too late yet.

CURTIS—[With a grin.] Thirty-nine candles, if you're thinking of baking a cake!

BIGELOW—[Meaningly.] That's not old—but it's not young either, Curt.

CURTIS—[Disgustedly.] You talk like an old woman, Big. What have years to do with it? Martha is young in spirit and always will be. [There is a knock at the door and MARTHA's voice calling: "May I come in, people? "] Sure thing! [BIGELOW jumps to open the door and MARTHA enters. She is flushed, excited, full of the joy of life, panting from her exertions.]

MARTHA—[Laughing.] I've had to run away and leave them with the governess. They're too active for me. [She throws herself on the couch.] Phew! I'm all tired out. I must be getting old.

CURTIS—[With a grin.] Big was just this minute remarking that, Martha. [BIGELOW looks embarrassed.]

MARTHA—[Laughing at him.] Well, I declare! Of all the horrid things to hear—

BIGELOW—[Still embarrassed but forcing a joking tone.] He—prevaricates, Mrs. Jayson.

MARTHA—There now, Curt! I'm sure it was you who said it. It sounds just like one of your horrid facts.

BIGELOW—And how can I offer my felicitations now? But I do, despite your husband's calumny. May your shadow never grow less!

MARTHA—Thank you. [She shakes his proffered hand heartily.]

BIGELOW—And now I'll collect my flock and go home.

CURTIS—So long, Big. Be sure you don't mislay one of your heirs!

BIGELOW—No fear—but they might mislay me. [He goes. CURT sits down on couch. MARTHA goes to the window right, and looks out— after a pause, waving her hand.]

MARTHA—There they go. What darlings they are! [CURTIS grunts perfunctorily. MARTHA comes back and sits beside CURT on the couch—with a sigh.] Whoever did say it was right, Curt, I am getting old.

CURTIS—[Taking one of her hands and patting it.] Nonsense!

MARTHA—[Shaking her head and smiling with a touch of sadness.] No. I feel it.

CURTIS—[Puts his arms around her protectingly.] Nonsense! You're not the sort that ever grows old.

MARTHA—[Nestling up to him.] I'm afraid we're all that sort, dear. Even you. [She touches the white hair about his temples playfully.] Circumstantial evidence. I'll have to dye it when you're asleep some time—and then nobody'll know.

CURTIS—[Looking at her.] You haven't any silver threads. [Jokingly.] Am I to suspect—?

MARTHA—No, I don't. Honest, cross my heart, I wouldn't even conceal that from you, if I did. But gray hairs prove nothing. I am actually older than you, don't forget.

CURTIS—One whole year! That's frightful, isn't it?

MARTHA—I'm a woman, remember; so that one means at least six. Ugh! Let's not talk about it. Do you know, it really fills me with a queer panic sometimes?

CURTIS—[Squeezing her.] Silly girl!

MARTHA—[Snuggling close to him.] Will you always love me—even when I'm old and ugly and feeble and you're still young and strong and handsome?

CURTIS—[Kisses her—tenderly.] Martha! What a foolish question, sweetheart. If we ever have to grow old, we'll do it together just as we've always done everything.

MARTHA—[With a happy sigh.] That's my dream of happiness, Curt. [Enthusiastically.] Oh, it has been a wonderful, strange life we've lived together, Curt, hasn't it? You're sure you've never regretted—never had the weest doubt that it might have been better with—someone else?

CURTIS—[Kisses her again—tenderly reproachful.] Martha!

MARTHA—And I have helped—really helped you, haven't I?

CURTIS—[Much moved.] You've been the best wife a man could ever wish for, Martha. You've been—you are wonderful. I owe everything to you—your sympathy and encouragement. Don't you know I realize that? [She kisses him gratefully.]

MARTHA—[Musing happily.] Yes, it's been a wonderful, glorious life. I'd live it over again if I could, every single second of it—even the terrible suffering—the children.

CURTIS—[Wincing.] Don't. I wouldn't want that over again. [Then changing the subject abruptly.] But why have you been putting all our life into the past tense? It seems to me the most interesting part is still ahead of us.

MARTHA—[Softly.] I mean—together—Curt.

CURTIS—So do I!

MARTHA—But you're going away—and I can't go with you this time.

CURTIS—[Smiling to himself over her head.] Yes, that does complicate matters, doesn't it?

MARTHA—[Hurt—looking up at him.] Curt! How indifferently you say that—as if you didn't care!

CURTIS—[Avoiding her eyes—teasingly.] What do you think you'll do all the time I'm gone?

MARTHA—Oh, I'll be lost—dead—I won't know what to do. I'll die of loneliness—[yearning creeping into her voice] unless—

CURTIS—[Inquisitively.] Unless what?

MARTHA—[Burying her face on his shoulder—passionately.] Oh, Curt, I love you so! Swear that you'll always love me no matter what I do—no matter what I ask—

CURTIS—[Vaguely uneasy now, trying to peer into her face.] But, sweetheart—

MARTHA—[Giving way weakly to her feelings for a moment—entreatingly.] Then don't go!

CURTIS—[Astonished.] Why, I've got to go. You know that.

MARTHA—Yes, I suppose you have. [Vigorously, as if flinging off a weakness.] Of course you have!

CURTIS—But, Martha—you said you'd be lonely unless—unless what?

Martha—Unless I—[She hesitates, blushing and confused.] I mean we—oh, I'm so afraid of what you'll—hold me close, very close to you and I'll whisper it. [She pulls his head down and whispers in his ear. A look of disappointment and aversion forces itself on his face.]

CURTIS—[Almost indignantly.] But that's impossible, Martha!

MARTHA—[Pleadingly.] Now don't be angry with me, Curt—not till you've heard everything. [With a trace of defiance.] It isn't impossible, Curt. It's so! It's happened! I was saving it as a secret—to tell you to-day—on my birthday.

CURTIS—[Stunned.] You mean it—is a fact?

MARTHA—Yes. [Then pitifully.] Oh, Curt, don't look that way! You seem so cold—so far away from me. [Straining her arms about him.] Why don't you hold me close to you? Why don't you say you're glad—for my sake?

CURTIS—[Agitatedly.] But Martha—you don't understand. How can I pretend gladness when—[Vehemently.] Why, it would spoil all our plans!

MARTHA—Plans? OUR plans? What do you mean?

CURTIS—[Excitedly.] Why, you're going with me, of course! I've obtained official permission. I've been working for it for months. The letter came yesterday morning.

MARTHA—[Stunned.] Permission—to go with you—

CURTIS—[Excitedly.] Yes. I couldn't conceive going without you. And I knew how you must be wishing—

MARTHA—[In pain.] Oh!

CURTIS—[Distractedly—jumping to his feet and staring at her bewilderedly.] Martha! You don't mean to tell me you weren't!

MARTHA—[In a crushed voice.] I was wishing you would finally decide not to go—to stay at home.

CURTIS—[Betraying exasperation.] But you must realize that's impossible. Martha, are you sure you've clearly understood what I've told you? You can go with me, do you hear? Everything is arranged. And I've had to fight so hard—I was running the risk of losing my own chance by my insistence that I couldn't go without you.

MARTHA—[Weakly and helplessly.] I understand all that, Curt.

CURTIS—[Indignantly.] And yet—you hesitate! Why, this is the greatest thing of its kind ever attempted! There are unprecedented possibilities! A whole new world of knowledge may be opened up—the very origin of Man himself! And you will be the only woman—

MARTHA—I realize all that, Curt.

CURTIS—You can't—and hesitate! And then—think, Martha! —it will mean that you and I won't have to be separated. We can go on living the old, free life together.

MARTHA—[Growing calm now.] You are forgetting—what I told you, Curt. You must face the fact. I cannot go.

CURTIS—[Overwhelmed by the finality of her tone—after a pause.] How long have you known—this?

MARTHA—Two months, about.

CURTIS—But why didn't you tell me before?

MARTHA—I was afraid you wouldn't understand—and you haven't, Curt. But why didn't you tell me before—what you were planning?

CURTIS—[Eagerly.] You mean—then—you would have been glad to go— before this had happened?

MARTHA—I would have accepted it.

CURTIS—[Despairingly.] Martha, how could you ever have allowed this to happen? Oh, I suppose I'm talking foolishness. It wasn't your seeking, I know.

MARTHA—Yes it was, Curt. I wished it. I sought it.

CURTIS—[Indignantly.] Martha! [Then in a hurt tone.] You have broken the promise we made when they died. We were to keep their memories inviolate. They were to be always—our only children.

MARTHA—[Gently.] They forgive me, Curt. And you will forgive me, too—when you see him—and love him.

CURTIS—Him?

MARTHA—I know it will be a boy.

CURTIS—[Sinking down on the couch beside her—dully.] Martha! You have blown my world to bits.

MARTHA—[Taking one of his hands in hers—gently.] You must make allowances for me. Curt, and forgive me. I AM getting old. No, it's the truth. I've reached the turning point. Will you listen to my side of it, Curt, and try to see it—with sympathy—with true understanding—[With a trace of bitterness.]—forgetting your work for the moment?

CURTIS—[Miserably.] That's unfair, Martha. I think of it as OUR work—and I have always believed you did, too.

MARTHA—[Quickly.] I did, Curt! I do! All in the past is our work. It's my greatest pride to think so. But, Curt, I'll have to confess frankly—during the past two years I've felt myself— feeling as if I wasn't complete—with that alone.

CURTIS—Martha! [Bitterly.] And all the time I believed that more and more it was becoming the aim of your life, too.

MARTHA—[With a sad smile.] I'm glad of that, dear. I tried my best to conceal it from you. It would have been so unfair to let you guess while we were still in harness. But oh, how I kept looking forward to the time when we would come back—and rest—in our own home! You know—you said that was your plan—to stay here and write your books—and I was hoping—

CURTIS—[With a gesture of aversion.] I loathe this book-writing. It isn't my part, I realize now. But when I made the plans you speak of, how could I know that then?

MARTHA—[Decisively.] You've got to go. I won't try to stop you. I'll help all in my power—as I've always done. Only—I can't go with you any more. And you must help me—to do my work—by understanding it. [He is silent, frowning, his face agitated, preoccupied. She goes on intensely.] Oh, Curt, I wish I could tell you what I feel, make you feel with me the longing for a child. If you had just the tiniest bit of feminine in you—! [Forcing a smile.] But you're so utterly masculine, dear! That's what has made me love you, I suppose—so I've no right to complain of it. [Intensely.] I don't. I wouldn't have you changed one bit! I love you! And I love the things you love—your work—because it's a part of you. And that's what I want you to do—to reciprocate—to love the creator in me—to desire that I, too, should complete myself with the thing nearest my heart!

CURTIS—[Intensely preoccupied with his own struggle—vaguely.] But I thought—

MARTHA—I know; but, after all, your work is yours, not mine. I have been only a helper, a good comrade, too, I hope, but—somehow—outside of it all. Do you remember two years ago when we were camped in Yunnan, among the aboriginal tribes? It was one night there when we were lying out in our sleeping-bags up in the mountains along the Tibetan frontier. I couldn't sleep. Suddenly I felt oh, so tired—utterly alone—out of harmony with you—with the earth under me. I became horribly despondent—like an outcast who suddenly realizes the whole world is alien. And all the wandering about the world, and all the romance and excitement I'd enjoyed in it, appeared an aimless, futile business, chasing around in a circle in an effort to avoid touching reality. Forgive me, Curt. I meant myself, not you, of course. Oh, it was horrible, I tell you, to feel that way. I tried to laugh at myself, to fight it off, but it stayed and grew worse. It seemed as if I were the only creature alive—who was not alive. And all at once the picture came of a tribeswoman who stood looking at us in a little mountain village as we rode by. She was nursing her child. Her eyes were so curiously sure of herself. She was horribly ugly, poor woman, and yet—as the picture came back to me—I appeared to myself the ugly one while she was beautiful. And I thought of our children who had died—and such a longing for another child came to me that I began sobbing. You were asleep. You didn't hear. [She pauses—then proceeds slowly.] And when we came back here—to have a home at last, I was so happy because I saw my chance of fulfillment—before it was too late. [In a gentle, pleading voice.] Now can you understand, dear? [She puts her hand on his arm.]

CURTIS—[Starting as if awaking from a sleep.] Understand? No, I can't understand, Martha.

MARTHA—[In a gasp of unbearable hurt.] Curt! I don't believe you heard a word I was saying.

CURTIS—[Bursting forth as if releasing all the pent-up struggle that has been gathering within him.] No, I can't understand. I cannot, cannot! It seems like treachery to me.

MARTHA—Curt!

CURTIS—I've depended on you. This is the crucial point—the biggest thing of my life—and you desert me!

MARTHA—[Resentment gathering in her eyes.] If you had listened to me—if you had even tried to feel—

CURTIS—I feel that you are deliberately ruining my highest hope. How can I go on without you? I've been trying to imagine myself alone. I can't! Even with my work—who can I get to take your place? Oh, Martha, why do you have to bring this new element into our lives at this late day? Haven't we been sufficient, you and I together? Isn't that a more difficult, beautiful happiness to achieve than—children? Everyone has children. Don't I love you as much as any man could love a woman? Isn't that enough for you? Doesn't it mean anything to you that I need you so terribly—for myself, for my work—for everything that is best and worthiest in me? Can you expect me to be glad when you propose to introduce a stranger who will steal away your love, your interest—who will separate us and deprive me of you! No, no, I cannot! It's asking the impossible. I am only human.

MARTHA—If you were human you would think of my life as well as yours.

CURTIS—I do! It is OUR life I am fighting for, not mine—OUR life that you want to destroy.

MARTHA—Our life seems to mean your life to you, Curt—and only your life. I have devoted fifteen years to that. Now I must fight for my own.

CURTIS—[Aghast.] You talk as if we were enemies, Martha! [Striding forward and seizing her in his arms.] No, you don't mean it! I love you so, Martha! You've made yourself part of my life, my work—I need you so! I can't share you with anyone! I won't! Martha, my own! Say that you won't, dear? [He kisses her passionately again and again.]

MARTHA—[All her love and tenderness aroused by his kisses and passionate sincerity—weakening.] Curt! Curt! [Pitiably.] It won't separate us, dear. Can't you see he will be a link between us— even when we are away from each other—that he will bring us together all the closer?

CURTIS—But I can't be away from you!

MARTHA—[Miserably.] Oh, Curt, why won't you look the fact in the face—and learn to accept it with joy? Why can't you for my sake? I would do that for you.

CURTIS—[Breaking away from her—passionately.] You will not do what I have implored you—for me! And I am looking the fact in the face—the fact that there must be no fact! [Avoiding her eyes—as if defying his own finer feelings.] There are doctors who—

MARTHA—[Shrinking back from him.] Curt! You propose that—to me! [With overwhelming sorrow.] Oh, Curt! When I feel him—his life within me—like a budding of my deepest soul—to flower and continue me—you say what you have just said! [Grief-stricken.] Oh, you never, never, never will understand!

CURTIS—[Shamefacedly.] Martha, I—[Distractedly.] I don't know what I'm saying! This whole situation is so unbearable! Why, why does it have to happen now?

MARTHA—[Gently.] It must be now—or not at all—at my age, dear. [Then after a pause—staring at him frightenedly—sadly.] You have changed, Curt. I remember it used to be your happiness to sacrifice yourself for me.

CURTIS—I had no work then—no purpose beyond myself. To sacrifice oneself is easy. But when your only meaning becomes as a searcher for knowledge—you cannot sacrifice that, Martha. You must sacrifice everything for that—or lose all sincerity.

MARTHA—I wonder where your work leaves off and you begin. Hasn't your work become you?

CURTIS—Yes and no. [Helplessly.] You can't understand, Martha!...

MARTHA—Nor you.

CURTIS—[With a trace of bitter irony.] And you and your work? Aren't they one and the same?

MARTHA—So you think mine is selfish, too? [After a pause—sadly.] I can't blame you, Curt. It's all my fault. I've spoiled you by giving up my life so completely to yours. You've forgotten I have one. Oh, I don't mean that I was a martyr. I know that in you alone lay my happiness and fulfillment in those years—after the children died. But we are no longer what we were then. We must, both of us, relearn to love and respect—what we have become.

CURTIS—[Violently.] Nonsense! You talk as if love were an intellectual process—[Taking her into his arms—passionately.] I love you—always and forever! You are me and I am you. What use is all this vivisecting? [He kisses her fiercely. They look into each other's eyes for a second—then instinctively fall back from one another.]

MARTHA—[In a whisper.] Yes, you love me. But who am I? There is no recognition in your eyes. You don't know.

CURTIS—[Frightenedly.] Martha! Stop! This is terrible! [They continue to be held by each other's fearfully questioning eyes.]

[The Curtain Falls]

ACT III

SCENE—Same as Act II. As the curtain rises, JAYSON is discovered sitting in an armchair by the fireplace, in which a log fire is burning fitfully. He is staring into the flames, a strained, expectant expression on his face. It is about three o'clock in the morning. There is no light but that furnished by the fire which fills the room with shifting shadows. The door in the rear is opened and RICHARD appears, his face harried by the stress of unusual emotion. Through the opened doorway, a low, muffled moan of anguish sounds from the upper part of the house. JAYSON and RICHARD both shudder. The latter closes the door behind him quickly as if anxious to shut out the noise.

JAYSON—[Looking up anxiously.] Well?

RICHARD—[Involuntarily straightening up as if about to salute and report to a superior officer.] No change, sir. [Then, as if remembering himself, comes to the fireplace and slumps down in a chair—agitatedly.] God, Dad, I can't stand her moaning and screaming! It's got my nerves shot to pieces. I thought I was hardened. I've heard them out in No Man's Land—dying by inches— when you couldn't get to them or help—but this is worse—a million times! After all, that was war—and they were men—

JAYSON—Martha is having an exceptionally hard ordeal.

RICHARD—Since three o'clock this morning—yesterday morning, I should say. It's a wonder she isn't dead.

JAYSON—[After a pause.] Where is Curt?

RICHARD—[Harshly.] Still out in the garden, walking around bareheaded in the cold like a lunatic.

JAYSON—Why didn't you make him come in?

RICHARD—Make him! It's easy to say. He's in a queer state, Dad, I can tell you! There's something torturing him besides her pain—

JAYSON—[After a pause.] Yes, there's a lot in all this we don't know about.

RICHARD—I suppose the reason he's so down on the family is because we've rather cut her since that tea affair.

JAYSON—He shouldn't blame us. She acted abominably and has certainly caused enough talk since then—always about with Bigelow—

RICHARD—[With a sardonic laugh.] And yet he keeps asking everyone to send for Bigelow—says he wants to talk to him—not us. WE can't understand! [He laughs bitterly.]

JAYSON—I'm afraid Curt knows we understand too much. [Agitatedly.] But why does he want Bigelow, in God's name? In his present state—with the suspicions he must have—there's liable to be a frightful scene.

RICHARD—Don't be afraid of a scene. [With pitying scorn.] The hell of it is he seems to regard Bigelow as his best friend. Damned if I can make it out.

JAYSON—I gave orders that they were always to tell Curt Bigelow was out of town and couldn't be reached. [With a sigh.] What a frightful situation for all of us! [After a pause.] It may sound cruel of me—but—I can't help wishing for all our sakes that this child will never—

RICHARD—Yes, Dad, I know what you're thinking. It would be the best thing for it, too—although I hate myself for saying it. [There is a pause. Then the door in rear is opened and LILY appears. She is pale and agitated. Leaving the door open behind her she comes forward and flings herself on the lounge.]

JAYSON—[Anxiously.] Well?

LILY—[Irritably, getting up and switching on the lights.] Isn't everything gloomy enough? [Sits down.] I couldn't bear it upstairs one second longer. Esther and Emily are coming down, too. It's too much for them—and they've had personal experience. [Trying to mask her agitation by a pretense at flippancy.] I hereby become a life-member of the birth-control league. Let's let humanity cease— if God can't manage its continuance any better than that!

RICHARD—[Seriously.] Second the motion.

JAYSON—[Peevishly.] You're young idiots. Keep your blasphemous nonsense to yourself, Lily!

LILY—[Jumping up and stamping her foot—hysterically.] I can't stand it. Take me home, Dick, won't you? We're doing no good waiting here. I'll have a fit—or something—if I stay.

RICHARD—[Glad of the excuse to go himself—briskly.] That's how I feel. I'll drive you home. Come along. [ESTHER and EMILY enter, followed by JOHN.]

LILY—[Excitedly.] I'll never marry or have a child! Never, never! I'll go into Mark's office to-morrow and make myself independent of marriage.

ESTHER—Sssh! Lily! Don't you know you're shouting? And what silly talk!

LILY—I'll show you whether it's silly! I'll—

RICHARD—[Impatiently.] Are you coming or not?

LILY—[Quickly.] Yes—wait—here I am. [She pushes past the others and follows RICHARD out rear. ESTHER and EMILY sit on couch—JOHN on chair, right rear.]

ESTHER—[With a sigh.] I thought I went through something when mine were born—but this is too awful.

EMILY—And, according to John, Curt actually says he hates it! Isn't that terrible? [After a pause—meaningly.] It's almost as if her suffering was a punishment, don't you think?

ESTHER—If it is, she's being punished enough, Heaven knows. It can't go on this way much longer or something dreadful will happen.

EMILY—Do you think the baby—

ESTHER—I don't know. I shouldn't say it but perhaps it would be better if—

EMILY—That's what I think.

ESTHER—Oh, I wish I didn't have such evil suspicions—but the way Curt goes on—how can you help feeling there's something wrong?

JAYSON—[Suddenly.] How is Curt?

EMILY—John just came in from the garden. [Turning around to where JOHN is dozing in his chair—sharply.] John! Well I never! If he isn't falling asleep! John! [He jerks up his head and stares at her, blinking stupidly. She continues irritably.] A nice time to pick out for a nap, I must say.

JOHN—[Surlily.] Don't forget I have to be at the bank in the morning.

JAYSON—[Testily.] I have to be at the bank, too—and you don't notice me sleeping. Tell me about Curt. You just left him, didn't you?

JOHN—[Irritably.] Yes, and I've been walking around that damned garden half the night watching over him. Isn't that enough to wear anyone out? I can feel I've got a terrible cold coming on—

ESTHER—[Impatiently.] For goodness sake, don't you start to pity yourself!

JOHN—[Indignantly.] I'm not. I think I've showed my willingness to do everything I could. If Curt was only the least bit grateful! He isn't. He hates us all and wishes we were out of his home. I would have left long ago if I didn't want to do my part in saving the family name from disgrace.

JAYSON—[Impatiently.] Has he quieted down, that's what I want to know?

JOHN—[Harshly.] Not the least bit. He's out of his head—and I'd be out of mine if a child was being born to my wife that—

JAYSON—[Angrily.] Keep that to yourself! Remember you have no proof. [Morosely.] Think all you want—but don't talk.

EMILY—[Pettishly.] The whole town knows it, anyway; I'm sure they must.

JAYSON—There's only been gossip—no real scandal. Let's do our united best to keep it at that. [After a pause.] Where's Aunt Elizabeth? We'll have to keep an eye on her, too, or she's quite liable to blurt out the whole business before all comers.

ESTHER—You needn't be afraid. She's forgotten all about the scandalous part. No word of it has come to her out in the country and she hasn't set foot in town since that unfortunate tea, remember. And at present she's so busy wishing the child will be a boy, that she hasn't a thought for another thing. [The door in the rear is opened and MARK SHEFFIELD enters. He comes up to the fire to warm himself. The others watch him in silence for a moment.]

JAYSON—[Impatiently.] Well, Mark? Where's Curt?

SHEFFIELD—[Frowning.] Inside. I think he'll be with us in a minute. [With a scornful smile.] Just now he's 'phoning to Bigelow. [The others gasp.]

JAYSON—[Furiously.] For God's sake, couldn't you stop him?

SHEFFIELD—Not without a scene. Your Aunt persuaded him to come into the house—and he rushed for the 'phone. I think he guessed we had been lying to him—

JAYSON—[After a pause.] Then he—Bigelow will be here soon?

SHEFFIELD—[Drily.] It depends on his sense of decency. As he seems lacking in that quality, I've no doubt he'll come.

JOHN—[Rising to his feet—pompously.] Then I, for one, will go. Come, Emily. Since Curt seems bound to disgrace everyone concerned, I want it thoroughly understood that we wash our hands of the whole disgraceful affair.

EMILY—[Snappishly.] Go if you want to! I won't! [Then with a sacrificing air.] I think it is our duty to stay.

JAYSON—[Exasperated.] Sit down. Wash your hands indeed! Aren't you as much concerned as any of us?

SHEFFIELD—[Sharply.] Sshh! I think I hear Curt now. [JOHN sits down abruptly. All stiffen into stony attitudes. The door is opened and CURT enters. He is incredibly drawn and haggard, a tortured, bewildered expression in his eyes. His hair is dishevelled, his boots caked with mud. He stands at the door staring from one to the other of his family with a wild, contemptuous scorn and mutters.]

CURTIS—Liars! Well, he's coming now. [Then bewilderedly.] Why didn't you want him to come, eh? He's my oldest friend. I've got to talk to someone—and I can't to you. [Wildly.] What do you want here, anyway? Why don't you go? [A scream of MARTHA's is heard through the doorway. CURT shudders violently, slams the door to with a crash, putting his shoulders against it as if to bar out the sound inexorably—in anguish.] God, why must she go through such agony? Why? Why? [He goes to the fireplace as MARK makes way for him, flings himself exhaustedly on a chair, his shoulders bowed, his face hidden in his hands. The others stare at him pityingly. There is a long silence. Then the two women whisper together, get up and tiptoe out of the room, motioning for the others to follow them. JOHN does so. SHEFFIELD starts to go, then notices the preoccupied JAYSON who is staring moodily into the fire.]

SHEFFIELD—Sstt! [As JAYSON looks up—in a whisper.] Let's go out and leave him alone. Perhaps he'll sleep.

JAYSON—[Starting to follow SHEFFIELD, hesitates and puts a hand on his son's shoulder.] Curt. Remember I'm your father. Can't you confide in me? I'll do anything to help.

CURTIS—[Harshly.] No, Dad. Leave me alone.

JAYSON—[Piqued.] As you wish. [He starts to go.]

CURTIS—And send Big in to me as soon as he comes.

JAYSON—[Stops, appears about to object—then remarks coldly.] Very well—if you insist. [He switches off the lights. He hesitates at the door uncertainly, then opens it and goes out. There is a pause. Then CURT lifts his head and peers about the room. Seeing he is alone he springs to his feet and begins to pace back and forth, his teeth clenched, his features working convulsively. Then, as if attracted by an irresistible impulse, he goes to the closed door and puts his ear to the crack. He evidently hears his wife's moans for he starts away—in agony.]

CURTIS—Oh, Martha, Martha! Martha, darling! [He flings himself in the chair by the fireplace—hides his face in his hands and sobs bitterly. There is a ring from somewhere in the house. Soon after there is a knock at the door. CURTIS doesn't hear at first but when it is repeated he mutters huskily.] Come in. [BIGELOW enters. CURT looks up at him.] Close that door, Big, for God's sake!

BIGELOW—[Does so—then taking off his overcoat, hat, and throwing them on the lounge comes quickly over to CURT.] I got over as soon as I could. [As he sees CURT's face he starts and says sympathetically.] By Jove, old man, you look as though you'd been through hell!

CURTIS—[Grimly.] I have. I am.

BIGELOW—[Slapping his back.] Buck up! [Then anxiously.] How's Martha?

CURTIS—She's in hell, too—

BIGELOW—[Attempting consolation.] You're surely not worrying, are you? Martha is so strong and healthy there's no doubt of her pulling through in fine shape.

CURTIS—She should never have attempted this. [After a pause.] I've a grudge against you, Big. It was you bringing your children over here that first planted this in her mind.

BIGELOW—[After a pause.] I've guessed you thought that. That's why you haven't noticed me—or them—over here so much lately. I'll confess that I felt you—[Angrily.] And the infernal gossip— I'll admit I thought that you—oh, damn this rotten town, anyway!

CURTIS—[Impatiently.] Oh, for God's sake! [Bitterly.] I didn't want you here to discuss Bridgetown gossip.

BIGELOW—I know, old man, forgive me. [In spite of the closed door one of MARTHA's agonized moans is heard. They both shudder.]

CURTIS—[In a dead, monotonous tone.] She has been moaning like that hour after hour. I shall have those sounds in my ears until the day I die. Nothing can ever make me forget—nothing.

BIGELOW—[Trying to distract him.] Deuce take it, Curt, what's the matter with you? I never thought you'd turn morbid.

CURTIS—[Darkly.] I've changed, Big—I hardly know myself any more.

BIGELOW—Once you're back on the job again, you'll be all right. You're still determined to go on this expedition, aren't you?

CURTIS—Yes. I was supposed to join them this week in New York but I've arranged to catch up with them in China—as soon as it's possible for us to go.

BIGELOW—Us? You mean you still plan to take—

CURTIS—[Angrily aggressive.] Yes, certainly! Why not? Martha ought to be able to travel in a month or so.

BIGELOW—Yes, but—do you think it would be safe to take the child?

CURTIS—[With a bitter laugh.] Yes—I was forgetting the child, wasn't I? [Viciously.] But perhaps—[Then catching himself with a groan.] Oh, damn all children, Big!

BIGELOW—[Astonished.] Curt!

CURTIS—[In anguish.] I can't help it—I've fought against it. But it's there—deep down in me—and I can't drive it out. I can't!

BIGELOW—[Bewildered.] What, Curt?

CURTIS—Hatred! Yes, hatred! What's the use of denying it? I must tell someone and you're the only one who might understand. [With a wild laugh.] For you—hated your wife, didn't you?

BIGELOW—[Stunned.] Good God, you don't mean you hate—Martha?

CURTIS—[Raging.] Hate Martha? How dare you, you fool! I love Martha—love her with every miserable drop of blood in me—with all my life—all my soul! She is my whole world—everything! Hate

Martha! God, man, have you gone crazy to say such a mad thing? [Savagely.] No. I hate it. It!

BIGELOW—[Shocked.] Curt! Don't you know you can't talk like that— now—when—CURTIS—[Harshly.] It has made us both suffer torments—not only now—every day, every hour, for months and months. Why shouldn't I hate it, eh?

BIGELOW—[Staring at his friend's wild, distorted face with growing horror.] Curt! Can't you realize how horrible—

CURTIS—Yes, it's horrible. I've told myself that a million times. [With emphasis.] But it's true!

BIGELOW—[Severely.] Shut up! You're not yourself. Come, think for a moment. What would Martha feel if she heard you going on this way? Why—it would kill her!

CURTIS—[With a sobbing groan.] Oh, I know, I know! [After a pause.] She read it in my eyes. Yes, it's horrible, but when I saw her there suffering so frightfully—I couldn't keep it out of my eyes. I tried to force it back—for her sake—but I couldn't. I was holding her hands and her eyes searched mine with such a longing question in them—and she read only my hatred there, not my love for her. And she screamed and seemed to try to push me away. I wanted to kneel down and pray for forgiveness—to tell her it was only my love for her—that I couldn't help it. And then the doctors told me to leave—and now the door is locked against me—[He sobs.]

BIGELOW—[Greatly moved.] This is only your damned imagination. They put you out because you were in their way, that's all. And as for Martha, she was probably suffering so much—

CURTIS—No. She read it in my eyes. I saw that look in hers—of horror—horror of me!

BIGELOW—[Gruffly.] You're raving, damn it!

CURTIS—[Unheeding.] It came home to her then—the undeniable truth. [With a groan.] Isn't it fiendish that I should be the one to add to her torture—in spite of myself—in spite of all my will to conceal it! She will never forgive me, never! And how can I forgive myself?

BIGELOW—[Distractedly.] For God's sake, don't think about it! It's absurd—ridiculous!

CURTIS—[Growing more calm—in a tone of obsession.] She's guessed it ever since that day when we quarreled—her birthday. Oh, you can have no idea of the misery there has been in our lives since then. You haven't seen or guessed the reason. No one has. It has been—the thought of IT.

BIGELOW—Curt!

CURTIS—[Unheeding.] For years we had welded our lives together so that we two were sufficient, each to each. There was no room for a third. And it was a fine, free life we had made—a life of new worlds, of discovery, of knowledge invaluable to mankind. Isn't such a life worth all the sacrifice it must entail?

BIGELOW—But that life was your life, Curt—

CURTIS—[Vehemently.] No, it was her life, too—her work as well as mine. She had made the life, our life—the work, our work. Had she the right to repudiate what she had built because she suddenly has a fancy for a home, children, a miserable ease! I had thought I was her home, her children. I had tried to make my life worthy of being that to her. And I had failed. I was not enough.

BIGELOW—Curt!

CURTIS—Oh, I tried to become reconciled. I tried my damnedest. I tried to love this child as I had loved those that died. But I couldn't. And so, this being estranged us. We loved as intensely as ever but IT pushed us apart. I grew to dread the idea of this intruder. She saw this in me. I denied it—but she knew. There was something in each of us the other grew to hate. And still we loved as never before, perhaps, for we grew to pity each other's helplessness.

BIGELOW—Curt! Are you sure you ought to tell anyone this?

CURTIS—[Waving his remark aside.] One day, when I was trying to imagine myself without her, and finding nothing but hopelessness—yet knowing I must go—a thought suddenly struck me—a horrible but fascinating possibility that had never occurred to me before. [With feverish intensity.] Can you guess what it was?

BIGELOW—No. And I think you've done enough morbid raving, if you ask me.

CURTIS—The thought that came to me was that if a certain thing happened, Martha could still go with me. And I knew, if it did happen, that she would want to go, that she would fling herself into the spirit of our work to forget, that she would be mine more than ever.

BIGELOW—[Afraid to believe the obvious answer.] Curt!

CURTIS—Yes. My thought was that the child might be born dead.

BIGELOW—[Repelled—sternly.] Damn it, man, do you know what you're saying? [Relentingly.] No, Curt, old boy, do stop talking. If you don't I'll send for a doctor, damned if I won't. That talk belongs in an asylum. God, man, can't you realize this is your child—yours as well as hers?

CURTIS—I've tried. I cannot. There is some inexorable force in me—

BIGELOW—[Coldly.] Do you realize how contemptible this confession makes you out? [Angrily.] Why, if you had one trace of human kindness in you—one bit of unselfish love for your wife—one particle of pity for her suffering—

CURTIS—[Anguished.] I have—all the love and pity in the world for her! That's why I can't help hating—the cause of her suffering.

BIGELOW—Have you never thought that you might repay Martha for giving up all her life to you by devoting the rest of yours to her?

CURTIS—[Bitterly.] She can be happy without me. She will have this child—to take my place. [Intensely.] You think I would not give up my work for her? But I would! I will stay here—do anything she wishes—if only we can make a new beginning again— together—ALONE!

BIGELOW—[Agitated.] Curt, for God's sake, don't return to that! Why, good God, man—even now—while you're speaking—don't you realize what may be happening? And you can talk as if you were wishing—

CURTIS—[Fiercely.] I can't help but wish it!

BIGELOW—[Distractedly.] For the love of God, if you have such thoughts, keep them to yourself. I won't listen! You make me despise life!

CURTIS—And would you have me love life? [The door in the rear is opened and JAYSON enters, pale and unnerved. A succession of quick, piercing shrieks is heard before he can close the door behind him. Shuddering.] My God! My God! [With a fierce cry.] Will—this—never—end!

JAYSON—[Tremblingly.] Sh-h-h, they say this is the crisis. [Puts his arm around CURT.] Bear up, my boy, it will soon be over now. [He sits down in the chair BIGELOW has vacated, pointedly ignoring the latter. The door is opened again and EMILY, ESTHER, JOHN and SHEFFIELD file in quickly as if escaping from the cries of the woman upstairs. They are all greatly agitated. CURT groans, pressing his clenched fists against his ears. The two women sit on the lounge. MARK comes forward and stands by JAYSON'S chair, JOHN sits by the door as before. BIGELOW retreats behind CURT's chair, aware of their hostility. There is a long pause.]

ESTHER—[Suddenly.] She has stopped—[They all listen.]

JAYSON—[Huskily.] Thank God, it's over at last. [The door is opened and MRS. DAVIDSON enters. The old lady is radiant, weeping tears of joy.]

MRS. DAVIDSON—[Calls out exultantly between sobs.] A son, Curt—a son. [With rapt fervor—falling on her knees.] Let us all give thanks to God!

CURTIS—[In a horrible cry of rage and anguish.] No! No! You lie! [They all cry out in fright and amazement: "CURT! " The door is opened and the NURSE appears.]

NURSE—[Looking at CURTIS, in a low voice.] Mr. Jayson, your wife is asking for you.

BIGELOW—[Promptly slapping CURT on the back.] There! What did I tell you? Run, you chump!

CURTIS—[With a gasp of joy.] Martha! Darling, I'm coming—[He rushes out after the NURSE.]

BIGELOW—[Comes forward to get his hat and coat from the sofa—coldly.] Pardon me, please. [They shrink away from him.]

EMILY—[As he goes to the door—cuttingly.] Some people seem to have no sense of decency!

BIGELOW—[Stung, stops at the door and looks from one to the other of them—bitingly.] No, I quite agree with you. [He goes out, shutting the door. They all gasp angrily.]

JOHN—Scoundrel!

JAYSON—[Testily—going to MRS. D., who is still on her knees praying.] Do get up, Aunt Elizabeth! How ridiculous! What a scene if anyone should see you like that. [He raises her to her feet and leads her to a chair by the fire. She obeys unresistingly, seemingly unaware of what she is doing.]

ESTHER—[Unable to restrain her jealousy.] So it's a boy.

EMILY—Did you hear Curt—how he yelled out "No"? It's plain as the nose on your face he didn't want—

ESTHER—How awful!

JOHN—Well, can you blame him?

EMILY—And the awful cheek of that Bigelow person—coming here—

ESTHER—They appeared as friendly as ever when we came in.

JOHN—[Scornfully.] Curt is a blind simpleton—and that man is a dyed-in-the-wool scoundrel.

JAYSON—[Frightenedly.] Shhh! Suppose we were overheard!

EMILY—When Curt leaves we can put her in her proper place. I'll soon let her know she hasn't fooled me, for one. [While she is speaking MRS. D. has gotten up and is going silently toward the door.]

JAYSON—[Testily.] Aunt Elizabeth, where are you going?

MRS. D.—[Tenderly.] I must see him again, the dear! [She goes out.]

ESTHER—[Devoured by curiosity—hesitatingly.] I think I—come on, Emily. Let's go up and see—

EMILY—Not I! I never want to lay eyes on it.

JOHN—Nor I.

ESTHER—I was only thinking—everyone will think it funny if we don't.

JAYSON—[Hastily.] Yes, yes. We must keep up appearances. [Getting to his feet.] Yes, I think we had better all go up—make some sort of inquiry about Martha, you know. It's expected of us and—[They are all standing, hesitating, when the door in the rear is opened and the NURSE appears, supporting CURT. The latter is like a corpse. His face is petrified with grief, his body seems limp and half-paralyzed.]

NURSE—[Her eyes flashing, indignantly.] It's a wonder some of you wouldn't come up—here, help me! Take him, can't you? I've got to run back!

[JAYSON and SHEFFIELD spring forward and lead CURT to a chair by the fire.]

JAYSON—[Anxious.] Curt! Curt, my boy! What is it, son?

EMILY—[Catching the NURSE as she tries to go.] Nurse! What is the matter?

NURSE—[Slowly.] His wife is dead. [They are all still, stunned.] She lived just long enough to recognize him.

EMILY—And—the baby?

NURSE—[With a professional air.] Oh, it's a fine, healthy baby—eleven pounds—that's what made it so difficult. [She goes. The others all stand in silence.]

ESTHER—[Suddenly sinking on the couch and bursting into tears.] Oh, I'm so sorry I said—or thought—anything wrong about her. Forgive me, Martha!

SHEFFIELD—[Honestly moved but unable to resist this opportunity for Latin—solemnly.] De mortuis nil nisi bonum.

JAYSON—[Who has been giving all his attention to his son.] Curt! Curt! EMILY—Hadn't the doctor better—

JAYSON—Shhh! He begins to recognize me. Curt!

CURTIS—[Looking around him bewilderedly.] Yes. [Suddenly remembrance comes and a spasm of intolerable pain contracts his features. He presses his hands to the side of his head and groans brokenly.] Martha! Gone! Dead! Oh! [He appeals wildly to the others.] Her eyes—she knew me—she smiled—she whispered—forgive me, Curt, —forgive her—when it was I who should have said forgive me—but before I could—she—[He falters brokenly.]

EMILY—[Looking from one to the other meaningly as if this justified all their suspicions.] Oh!

CURTIS—[A sudden triumph in his voice.] But she loved me again— only me—I saw it in her eyes! She had forgotten—IT. [Raging.] Never let me see it! Never let it come near me! It has murdered her! [Springing to his feet.] I hate it from the bottom of my soul—I will never see it—never—never—I take my oath! [As his father takes his arm—shaking him off.] Let me go! I am going back to her! [He strides out of the door in a frenzy of grief and rage. They all stand transfixed, looking at each other bewilderedly.]

EMILY—[Putting all her venomous gratification into one word.] Well!

[The Curtain Falls]

ACT IV

SCENE—Same as Act I. It is afternoon of a fine day three days later. Motors are heard coming up the drive in front of the house. There is the muffled sound of voices. The MAID is seen going along the hall to the front door. Then the family enter from the rear. First come JAYSON and ESTHER with MRS. DAVIDSON—then LILY, DICK and SHEFFIELD—then JOHN and his wife. All are dressed in mourning. The only one who betrays any signs of sincere grief is MRS. DAVIDSON. The others all have a strained look, irritated, worried, or merely gloomy. They seem to be thinking "The worst is yet to come."

JAYSON—[Leading MRS. D., who is weeping softly, to the chair at left of table—fretfully.] Please do sit down, Aunt. [She does so mechanically.] And do stop crying. [He sits down in front of table. ESTHER goes to couch where she is joined by EMILY. MARK goes over and stands in back of them. DICK and JOHN sit at rear of table. LILY comes down front and walks about nervously. She seems in a particularly fretful, upset mood.]

LILY—[Trying to conceal her feelings under a forced flippancy.] What ridiculous things funerals are, anyway! That stupid minister—whining away through his nose! Why does the Lord show such a partiality for men with adenoids, I wonder.

JAYSON—[Testily.] Sshhh! Have you no respect for anything?

LILY—[Resentfully.] If I had, I'd have lost it when I saw all of you pulling such long faces in the church where you knew you were under observation. Pah! Such hypocrisy! And then, to cap it all, Emily has to force out a few crocodile tears at the grave!

EMILY—[Indignantly.] When I saw Curt—that's why I cried—not for her!

JAYSON—What a scene Curt made! I actually believe he wanted to throw himself into the grave!

DICK—You BELIEVE he wanted to! Why, it was all Mark and I could do to hold him, wasn't it, Mark? [SHEFFIELD nods.]

JAYSON—Intolerable! I never expected he'd turn violent like that. He's seemed calm enough the past three days.

LILY—Calm! Yes, just like a corpse is calm!

JAYSON—[Distractedly.] And now this perfectly mad idea of going away to-day to join that infernal expedition—leaving that child on our hands—the child he has never even looked at! Why, it's too monstrously flagrant! He's deliberately flaunting this scandal in everyone's face!

JOHN—[Firmly.] He must be brought to time.

SHEFFIELD—Yes, we must talk to him—quite openly, if we're forced to. After all, I guess he realizes the situation more keenly than any of us.

LILY—[Who has wandered to window on right.] You mean you think he believes—Well, I don't. And you had better be careful not to let him guess what you think. [Pointing outside.] There's my proof. There he is walking about with Bigelow. Can you imagine Curt doing that—if he thought for a moment—

DICK—Oh, I guess Curt isn't all fool. He knows that's the very best way to keep people from suspecting.

ESTHER—[Indignantly.] But wouldn't you think that Bigelow person— It's disgusting, his sticking to Curt like this.

SHEFFIELD—Well, for one, I'm becoming quite resigned to Bigelow's presence. In the first place, he seems to be the only one who can bring Curt to reason. Then again, I feel that it is to Bigelow's own interest to convince Curt that he mustn't provoke an open scandal by running away without acknowledging this child.

LILY—[Suddenly bursting forth hysterically.] Oh, I hate you, all of you! I loathe your suspicions—and I loathe myself because I'm beginning to be poisoned by them, too.

EMILY—Really, Lily, at this late hour—after the way Curt has acted—and her last words when she was dying—

LILY—[Distractedly.] I know! Shut up! Haven't you told it a million times already? [MRS. DAVIDSON gets up and walks to the door, rear. She has been crying softly during this scene, oblivious to the talk around her.]

JAYSON—[Testily.] Aunt Elizabeth! Where are you going? [As she doesn't answer but goes out into the hall.] Esther, go with her and see that she doesn't—

ESTHER—[Gets up with a jealous irritation.] She's only going up to see the baby. She's simply forgotten everything else in the world!

LILY—[Indignantly.] She probably realizes what we are too mean to remember—that the baby, at least, is innocent. Wait, Esther. I'll come with you.

JAYSON—Yes, hurry, she shouldn't be left alone. [ESTHER and LILY follow the old lady out, rear.]

DICK—[After a pause—impatiently.] Well, what next? I don't see what good we are accomplishing. May I run along? [He gets up restlessly as he is speaking and goes to the window.]

JAYSON—[Severely.] You will stay, if you please. There's to be no shirking on anyone's part. It may take all of us to induce Curt—

SHEFFIELD—I wouldn't worry. Bigelow is taking that job off our hands, I imagine.

DICK—[Looking out of the window.] He certainly seems to be doing his damnedest. [With a sneer.] The stage missed a great actor in him.

JAYSON—[Worriedly.] But, if Bigelow should fail—

SHEFFIELD—Then we'll succeed. [With a grim smile.] By God, we'll have to.

JAYSON—Curt has already packed his trunks and had them taken down to the station—told me he was leaving on the five o'clock train.

SHEFFIELD—But didn't you hint to him there was now this matter of the child to be considered in making his plans?

JAYSON—[Lamely.] I started to. He simply flared up at me with insane rage.

DICK—[Looking out the window.] Say, I believe they're coming in.

JAYSON—Bigelow?

DICK—Yes, they're both making for the front door.

SHEFFIELD—I suggest we beat a retreat to Curt's study and wait there.

JAYSON—Yes, let's do that—come on, all of you. [They all retire grumblingly but precipitately to the study, closing the door behind them. The front door is heard opening and a moment later CURT and BIGELOW enter the room. CURT's face is set in an expression of stony grief. BIGELOW is flushed, excited, indignant.]

BIGELOW—[As CURT sinks down on the couch—pleading indignantly.] Curt, damn it, wake up! Are you made of stone? Has everything I've said gone in one ear and out the other? I know it's hell for me to torment you at this particular time but it's your own incredibly unreasonable actions that force me to. I know how terribly you must feel but—damn it, man, postpone this going away! Face this situation like a man! Be reconciled to your child, stay with him at least until you can make suitable arrangements—

CURTIS—[Fixedly.] I will never see it! Never!

BIGELOW—How can you keep repeating that—with Martha hardly cold in her grave! I ask you again, what would she think, how would she feel—If you would only consent to see this baby, I know you'd realize how damnably mad and cruel you are. Won't you—just for a second?

CURTIS—No. [Then raging.] If I saw it I'd be tempted to—[Then brokenly.] No more of that talk, Big. I've heard enough. I've reached the limit.

BIGELOW—[Restraining his anger with difficulty—coldly.] That's your final answer, eh? Well, I'm through. I've done all I could. If you want to play the brute—to forget all that was most dear in the world to Martha—to go your own damn selfish way—well, there's nothing more to be said. You will be punished for it, believe me! [He takes a step toward the door.] And I—I want you to understand that all friendship ceases between us from this day. You are not the Curt I thought I knew—and I have nothing but a feeling of repulsion—good-by. [He starts for the door.]

CURTIS—[Dully.] Good-by, Big.

BIGELOW—[Stops, his features working with grief and looks back at his friend—then suddenly goes back to him—penitently.] Curt! Forgive me! I ought to know better. This isn't you. You'll come to yourself when you've had time to think it over. The memory of Martha—she'll tell you what you must do. [He wrings CURT's hand.] Good-by, old scout!

CURTIS—[Dully.] Good-by. [BIGELOW hurries out, rear. CURT sits in a dumb apathy for a while—then groans heart-brokenly.] Martha! Martha! [He springs to his feet distractedly. The door of the study is slowly opened and SHEFFIELD peers out cautiously—then comes into the room, followed by the others. They all take seats as before. CURT ignores them.]

SHEFFIELD—[Clearing his throat.] Curt—

CURTIS—[Suddenly.] What time is it, do you know!

SHEFFIELD—[Looking at his watch.] Two minutes to four.

CURTIS—[Impatiently.] Still an hour more of this!

JAYSON—[Clearing his throat.] Curt—[Before he starts what he intends to say, there is the sound of voices from the hall. ESTHER and LILY help in MRS. DAVIDSON to her former chair. The old lady's face is again transformed with joy. ESTHER joins EMILY on the couch. LILY sits in chair—front right. There is a long, uncomfortable pause during which CURT paces up and down.]

MRS. DAVIDSON—[Suddenly murmuring aloud to herself—happily.] He's such a dear! I could stay watching him forever.

JAYSON—[Testily.] Sshhh! Aunt! [Then clearing his throat again.] Surely you're not still thinking of going on the five o'clock train, are you, Curt?

CURTIS—Yes.

SHEFFIELD—[Drily.] Then Mr. Bigelow didn't persuade you—

CURTIS—[Coldly and impatiently.] I'm not to be persuaded by Big or anyone else. And I'll thank you not to talk any more about it. [They all stiffen resentfully at his tone.]

JAYSON—[To CURT—in a pleading tone.] You mustn't be unreasonable, Curt. After all we are your family—your best friends in the world—and we are only trying to help you—

CURTIS—[With nervous vehemence.] I don't want your help. You will help me most by keeping silent.

EMILY—[With a meaning look at the others—sneeringly.] Yes, no doubt.

ESTHER—Sshhh, Emily!

JAYSON—[Helplessly.] But, you see, Curt—

SHEFFIELD—[With his best judicial air.] If you'll all allow me to be the spokesman, I think perhaps that I—[They all nod and signify their acquiescence.] Well, then, will you listen to me, Curt? [This last somewhat impatiently as CURT continues to pace, eyes on the floor.]

CURTIS—[Without looking at him—harshly.] Yes, I'm listening. What else can I do when you've got me cornered? Say what you like and let's get this over.

SHEFFIELD—First of all, Curt, I hope it is needless for me to express how very deeply we all feel for you in your sorrow. But we sincerely trust that you are aware of our heartfelt sympathy. [They all nod. A bitter, cynical smile comes over LILY's face.]

ESTHER—[Suddenly breaking down and beginning to weep.] Poor Martha! [SHEFFIELD glances at his wife, impatient at this interruption. The others also show their irritation.]

EMILY—[Pettishly.] Esther! For goodness sake! [CURT hesitates, stares at his sister frowningly as if judging her sincerity—then bends down over her and kisses the top of her bowed head impulsively—seems about to break down himself—grits his teeth and forces it back—glances around at the others defiantly and resumes his pacing. ESTHER dries her eyes, forcing a trembling smile. The cry has done her good.]

SHEFFIELD—[Clearing his throat.] I may truthfully say we all feel—as Esther does—even if we do not give vent—[With an air of sincere sympathy.] I know how terrible a day this must be for you, Curt. We all do. And we feel guilty in breaking in upon the sanctity of your sorrow in any way. But, if you will pardon my saying so, your own course of action—the suddenness of your plans—have made it imperative that we come to an understanding about certain things—about one thing in particular, I might say. [He pauses. CURT goes on pacing back and forth as if he hadn't heard.]

JAYSON—[Placatingly.] Yes, it is for the best, Curt.

ESTHER—Yes, Curt dear, you mustn't be unreasonable.

DICK—[Feeling called upon to say something.] Yes, old man, you've got to face things like a regular. Facts are facts. [This makes everybody uneasy.]

LILY—[Springing to her feet.] Phew! it's close in here. I'm going out in the garden. You can call me when these—orations—are finished. [She sweeps out scornfully.]

JAYSON—[Calling after her imperiously.] Lily! [But she doesn't answer and he gives it up with a hopeless sigh.]

CURTIS—[Harshly.] What time is it?

SHEFFIELD—You have plenty of time to listen to what I—I should rather say we—have to ask you, Curt. I promise to be brief. But first let me again impress upon you that I am talking in a spirit of the deepest friendliness and sympathy with you—as a fellow- member of the same family, I may say—and with the highest ideals and the honor of that family always in view. [CURT makes no comment. SHEFFIELD unconsciously begins to adopt the alert keenness of the cross-examiner.] First, let me ask you, is it your intention to take that five o'clock train to-day?

CURTIS—[Harshly.] I've told you that.

SHEFFIELD—And then you'll join this expedition to Asia?

CURTIS—You know that.

SHEFFIELD—To be gone five years?

CURTIS—[Shrugging his shoulders.] More or less.

SHEFFIELD—Is it your intention to return here at any time before you leave for Asia?

CURTIS—No!

SHEFFIELD—And your determination on these plans is irrevocable?

CURTIS—Irrevocable! Exactly. Please remember that.

SHEFFIELD—[Sharply.] That being your attitude, I will come bluntly to the core of the whole matter—the child whose coming into the world cost Martha her life.

CURTIS—[Savagely.] Her murderer! You are right! [They all look shocked, suspicious.]

SHEFFIELD—[Remonstratingly but suspiciously.] You can hardly hold the child responsible for the terrible outcome. Women die every day from the same cause. [Keenly.] Why do you attribute guilt to the child in this case, Curt?

CURTIS—It lives and Martha is gone—But, enough! I've said I never wanted it mentioned to me. Will you please remember that?

SHEFFIELD—[Sharply.] Its name is Jayson. Curt—in the eyes of the law. Will YOU please remember that?

CURTIS—[Distractedly.] I don't want to remember anything! [Wildly.] Please, for God's sake, leave me alone!

SHEFFIELD—[Coldly.] I am sorry, Curt, but you cannot act as if you were alone in this affair.

CURTIS—Why not? Am I not alone—more alone this minute than any creature on God's earth?

SHEFFIELD—[Soothingly.] In your great grief. Yes, yes, of course. We all appreciate—and we hate to—[Persuasively.] Yes, it would be much wiser to postpone these practical considerations until you are in a calmer mood. And if you will only give us the chance—why not put off this precipitate departure—for a month, say—and in the meantime—

CURTIS—[Harshly.] I am going when I said I was. I must get away from this horrible hole—as far away as I can. I must get back to my work for only in it will I find Martha again. But you—you can't understand that. What is the good of all this talking which leads nowhere?

SHEFFIELD—[Coldly.] You're mistaken. It leads to this: Do you understand that your running away from this child—on the very day of its mother's funeral! —will have a very queer appearance in the eyes of the world?

EMILY—And what are you going to do with the baby, Curt? Do you think you can run off regardless and leave it here—on our hands?

CURTIS—[Distractedly.] I'll give it this home. And someone—anyone—Esther, Lily—can appoint a nurse to live here and—[Breaking down.] Oh, don't bother me!

SHEFFIELD—[Sharply.] In the world's eyes, it will appear precious like a desertion on your part.

CURTIS—Oh, arrange it to suit yourselves—anything you wish—

SHEFFIELD—[Quickly.] I'll take you at your word. Then let us arrange it this way. You will remain here a month longer at least—

CURTIS—No!

SHEFFIELD—[Ignoring the interruption.] You can make plans for the child's future in that time, become reconciled to it—

CURTIS—No!

JAYSON—[Pleadingly.] Curt—please—for all our sakes—when the honor of the family is at stake.

DICK—Yes, old man, there's that about it, you know.

CURTIS—No!

EMILY—Oh, he's impossible!

SHEFFIELD—Perhaps Curt misunderstood me. [Meaningly.] Be reconciled to it in the eyes of the public, Curt. That's what I meant. Your own private feelings in the matter—are no one's business but your own, of course.

CURTIS—[Bewilderedly.] But—I don't see—Oh, damn your eyes of the public!

EMILY—[Breaking in.] It's all very well for you to ignore what people in town think—you'll be in China or heaven knows where. The scandal won't touch you—but we've got to live here and have our position to consider.

CURTIS—[Mystified.] Scandal? What scandal? [Then with a harsh laugh.] Oh, you mean the imbecile busy-bodies will call me an unnatural father. Well, let them! I suppose I am. But they don't know—

EMILY—[Spitefully.] Perhaps they know more than you think they do.

CURTIS—[Turning on her—sharply.] Just what do you mean by that, eh?

ESTHER—Emily! Shhh!

JAYSON—[Flurriedly.] Be still, Emily. Let Mark do the talking.

SHEFFIELD—[Interposing placatingly.] What Emily means is simply this, Curt: You haven't even been to look at this child since it has been born—not once, have you?

CURTIS—No, and I never intend—

SHEFFIELD—[Insinuatingly.] And don't you suppose the doctors and nurses—and the servants—have noticed this? It is not the usual procedure, you must acknowledge, and they wouldn't be human if they didn't think your action—or lack of action—peculiar and comment on it outside.

CURTIS—Well, let them! Do you think I care a fiddler's curse how people judge me?

SHEFFIELD—It is hardly a case of their judging—you. [Breaking off as he catches CURT'S tortured eyes fixed on him wildly.] This is a small town, Curt, and you know as well as I do, gossip is not the least of its faults. It doesn't take long for such things to get started. [Persuasively.] Now I ask you frankly, is it wise to provoke deliberately what may easily be set at rest by a little— I'll be frank—a little pretense on your part?

JAYSON—Yes, my boy. As a Jayson, I know you don't wish—

ESTHEE—[With a sigh.] Yes, you really must think of us, Curt.

CURTIS—[In an acute state of muddled confusion.] But—I—you—how are you concerned? Pretense? You mean you want me to stay and pretend—in order that you won't be disturbed by any silly tales they tell about me? [With a wild laugh.] Good God, this is too much! Why does a man have to be maddened by fools at such a time! [Raging.] Leave me alone! You're like a swarm of poisonous flies.

JAYSON—Curt! This is—really—when we've tried to be so considerate—

JOHN—[Bursting with rage.] It's an outrage to allow such insults!

DICK—You're not playing the game, Curt.

EMILY—[Spitefully.] It seems to me it's much more for Martha's sake, we're urging you than for our own. After all, the town can't say anything against us.

CURTIS—[Turning on her.] Martha's sake? [Brokenly.] Martha is gone. Leave her out of this.

SHEFFIELD—[Sharply.] But unfortunately, Curt, others will not leave her out of this. They will pry and pry—you know what they are—and—

EMILY—Curt couldn't act the way he is doing if he ever really cared for her.

CURTIS—You dare to say that! [Then controlling himself a bit—with scathing scorn.] What do know of love—women like you! You call your little rabbit-hutch emotions love—your bread-and- butter passions—and you have the effrontery to judge—

EMILY—[Shrinking from him frighteningly.] Oh! John!

JOHN—[Getting to his feet.] I protest! I cannot allow even my own brother—

DICK—[Grabbing his arm.] Keep your head, old boy.

SHEFFIELD—[Peremptorily.] You are making a fool of yourself, Curt—and you are damned insulting in the bargain. I think I may say that we've all about reached the end of our patience. What Emily said is for your own best interest, if you had the sense to see it. And I put it to you once and for all: Are you or are you not willing to act like a man of honor to protect your own good name, the family name, the name of this child, and your wife's memory? Let me tell you, your wife's good name is more endangered by your stubbornness than anything else.

CURTIS—[Trembling with rage.] I—I begin to think—you—all of you—are aiming at something against Martha in this. Yes—in back of your words—your actions—I begin to feel—[Raging.] Go away! Get out of this house—all of you! Oh, I know your meanness! I've seen how you've tried to hurt her ever since we came—because you resented in your small minds her evident superiority—

EMILY—[Scornfully.] Superiority, indeed!

CURTIS—Her breadth, of mind and greatness of soul that you couldn't understand. I've guessed all this, and if I haven't interfered it's only because I knew she was too far above you to notice your sickening malice—

EMILY—[Furiously.] You're only acting—acting for our benefit because you think we don't—

CURTIS—[Turning on her—with annihilating contempt.] Why, you— you poor little nonentity! [John struggles to get forward but Dick holds him back.]

EMILY—[Insane with rage—shrilly.] But we know—and the whole town knows—and you needn't pretend you've been blind. You've given the whole thing away yourself—the silly way you've acted—telling everyone how you hated that baby—letting everyone see—

JAYSON—Emily! [The others are all frightened, try to interrupt her. CURT stares at her in a stunned bewilderment]

EMILY—[Pouring forth all her venom regardless.] But you might as well leave off your idiotic pretending. It doesn't fool us—or anyone else—your sending for Bigelow that night—your hobnobbing with him ever since—your pretending he's as much your friend as ever. They're all afraid of you—but I'm not! I tell you to your face—it's all acting you're doing—just cheap acting to try and pull the wool over our eyes until you've run away like a coward— and left us to face the disgrace for you with this child on our hands!

ESTHER—[Trying to silence her—excitedly.] Emily! Keep still, for Heaven's sake! [The others all utter exclamations of caution, with fearful glances at CURT.]

EMILY—[Becoming exhausted by her outburst—more faintly.] Well, someone had to show him his place. He thinks he's so superior to us just because—telling us how much better she was than—But I won't stand for that. I've always had a clean name—and always will—and my children, too, thank God! [She sinks down on the couch exhausted, panting but still glaring defiantly at CURT.]

CURTIS—[An awareness of her meaning gradually forcing itself on his mind.] Bigelow! Big? Pretending he's as much my friend—[With a sudden gasp of sickened understanding.] Oh! [He sways as if he were about to fall, shrinking away from EMILY, all horror.] Oh, you—you—you-filth!

JOHN—[His fists clenched, tries to advance on his brother.] How dare you insult my wife! [He is restrained, held bake by his remonstrating father and DICK.]

MRS. DAVIDSON—[As if suddenly coming out of a dream—frightenedly.] What is the matter? Why is John mad at Curt?

CURTIS—[His hands over his eyes, acting like a person stricken with a sudden attack of nausea, weakly.] So—that's—what has been in your minds. Oh, this is bestial—disgusting! And there is nothing to be done. I feel defenseless. One would have to be as low as you are—She would have been defenseless, too. It is better she is dead. [He stares about him—wildly.] And you think—you all think—

ESTHER—[Pityingly.] Curt, dear, we don't think anything except what you've made us think with your crazy carrying-on.

CURTIS—[Looking from one to the other of them.] Yes—all of you— it's on your faces. [His eyes fix themselves on his aunt.] No, you don't—you don't—

MRS. DAVIDSON—I? Don't what, Curtis? My, how sick you look, poor boy!

CURTIS—You—don't believe—this child—

MRS. DAVIDSON—He's the sweetest baby I ever saw [proudly] and Jayson right to the tips of his toes.

CURTIS—Ah, I know you—[Looking around at the others with loathing and hatred.] But look at them—[With a burst of fierce determination.] Wait! I'll give you the only answer—[He dashes for the door in rear, shakes off his father and DICK, who try to stop him, and then is heard bounding up the stairs in hall. DICK runs after him, JAYSON as far as the doorway. ESTHER gives a stifled scream. There is a tense pause. Then DICK reappears.]

DICK—It's all right. I saw him go in.

JAYSON—[Frightenedly.] But—good God—he's liable—why didn't you follow him?

DICK—The doctor and nurse are there. They would have called out, wouldn't they, if—

MRS. DAVIDSON—[Getting angrier and angrier as her puzzlement has grown greater—in a stern tone.] I understand less and less of this. Where has Curtis gone? Why did he act so sick? What is the matter with all of you?

ESTHER—Nothing, Aunt dear, nothing!

MRS. DAVIDSON—No, you'll not hush me up! [Accusingly.] You all look guilty. Have you been saying anything against Curtis' baby? That was what Curtis seemed to think. A fine time you've picked out—with his wife not cold in her grave!

JAYSON—Aunt!

MRS. DAVIDSON—I never liked that woman. I never understood her. But now—now I love her and beg her forgiveness. She died like a true woman in the performance of her duty. She died gloriously—and I will always respect her memory. [Suddenly flying into a passion.] I feel that you are all hostile to her baby—poor, little, defenseless creature! Yes, you'd hate the idea of Curtis' having a son—you and your girls! Well, I'll make you bitterly regret the day you—[She plumps herself down in her chair again, staring stubbornly and angrily before her.]

EMILY—[Spitefully.] I fear it will be necessary to tell Aunt—

JAYSON—Sshh! You have made enough trouble with your telling already! [Miserably.] It should never have come to this pass. Curt will never forgive us, never!

ESTHER—[Resentfully to EMILY.] See what not holding your tongue has done—and my children will have to suffer for it, too!

SHEFFIELD—[Severely.] If Emily had permitted me to conduct this business uninterruptedly, this would never have occurred.
EMILY—That's right! All pick on me! Cowards! [She breaks down and sobs.]

DICK—[From the doorway. Coming back into the room.] Sstt! Here he comes!

CURTIS—[Reenters. There is a look of strange exultation on his face. He looks from one to the other of them. He stammers.] Well— my answer to you—your rotten world—I kissed him—he is mine! He looked at me—it was as if Martha looked at me—through his eyes.

ESTHER—[Voicing the general relief. Joyfully.] Oh, Curt! You won't go now? You'll stay?

CURTIS—[Staring at her, then from one to another of the rest with a withering scorn.] Ha! Now you think you have conquered, do you? No, I'm not going to stay! Do you think your vile slander could influence me to give up my work? And neither shall you influence the life of my son. I leave him here. I must. But not to your tender mercies. No, no! Thank God, there still remains one Jayson with unmuddled integrity to whom I can appeal. [He goes to MRS. DAVIDSON.] I will leave him in your care, Aunt—while I am gone.

MRS. DAVIDSON—[Delighted.] It will be a great happiness. He will be—the one God never granted me. [Her lips trembling.] God has answered my prayer at last.

CURTIS—I thank you, Aunt. [Kisses her reverentially.]

MRS. DAVIDSON—[Pleased but morally bound to grumble at him] But I cannot approve of your running away like this. It isn't natural. [Then with selfish haste, fearing her words may change his mind and she will lose the baby.] But you always were a queer person— and a man must do faithfully the work ordained for him.

CURTIS—[Gladly.] Yes, I must go! What would I be for him—or anyone—if I stayed? Thank God, you understand. But I will come back. [The light of an ideal beginning to shine in his eyes.] When he is old enough, I will teach him to know and love a big, free life. Martha used to say that he would take her part in time. My goal shall be his goal, too. Martha shall live again for me in him. And you, Aunt, swear to keep him with you—out there in the country—never to let him know this obscene little world. [He indicates his relatives.]

MRS. DAVIDSON—Yes, I promise, Curtis. Let anyone dare—! [She glares about her. The noise of a motor is heard from the drive. It stops in front of the house.]

CURTIS—I must go. [He kisses his aunt.] Teach him his mother was the most beautiful soul that ever lived. Good-by, Aunt.

MRS. DAVIDSON—Good-by, Curtis! [Without looking at the others, he starts for the door, rear. They all break out into conscience-stricken protestations.]

JAYSON—[Miserably.] Curt! You're not leaving us that way?

ESTHER—Curt—you're going—without a word! [They all say this practically together and crowd toward him. JOHN and EMILY remain sullenly apart. CURT turns to face them.]

LILY—[Enters from the rear.] You're not going, Curt?

CURTIS—[Turning to her.] Yes. Good-by, Lily. [He kisses her.] You loved her, didn't you? You are not like—Take my advice and get away before you become—[He has been staring into her face. Suddenly he pushes her brusquely away from him—coldly.] But I see in your face it's too late.

LILY—[Miserably.] No, Curt—I swear—

CURTIS—[Facing them all defiantly.] Yes, I am going without a word—because I cannot find the fitting one. Be thankful I can't. It would shrivel up your souls like flame, [He again turns and strides to the door.]

JAYSON—[His grief overcoming him.] My boy! We are wrong—we know— but—at least say you forgive us.

CURTIS—[Wavers with his back towards them—then turns and forces the words out.] Ask forgiveness of her. She—yes—she was so fine— I feel she—so you are forgiven. Good-by. [He goes. The motor is heard driving off. There is a tense pause.]

LILY—Then he did find out? Oh, a fine mess you've made of everything! But no—I should say "we, " shouldn't I? Curt guessed that. Oh, I hate you—and myself! [She breaks down.]
[There is a strained pause during which they are all silent, their eyes avoiding each other, fixed in dull, stupid stares. Finally, DICK fidgets uncomfortably, heaves a noisy sigh, and blurts out with an attempt at comforting reassurance:]

DICK—Well, it isn't as bad as it might have been, anyway. He did acknowledge the kid—before witnesses, too.

JAYSON—[Testily.] Keep your remarks to yourself, if you please! [But most of his family are already beginning to look relieved.]

[The Curtain Falls]

Printed in the United States
151079LV00005B/17/A

9 781406 532067